Saints and non-Saints

Saints and non-Saints

Christa Habegger

Ambassador International
GREENVILLE, SOUTH CAROLINA & BELFAST, NORTHERN IRELAND

SAINTS AND NON-SAINTS

ISBN 978 1 932307 82 5

Cover Design & Page Layout by
David Siglin of A&E Media

Published by the Ambassador Group

Ambassador International
427 Wade Hampton Blvd.
Greenville, SC 29609, USA
www.emeraldhouse.com

Ambassador Productions Ltd.
Providence House
Ardenlee Street
Belfast
BT6 8QJ
Northern Ireland
www.ambassador_productions.com

To my pastor, Dr. Alan Cairns, minister emeritus of Faith Free Presbyterian Church, an Ulsterman who encouraged me to study Patrick of Ireland, thus sparking my interest in the lives of the Saints, and to the memory of Dr. Bob Jones, Jr., who commissioned the project.

Special thanks to Sam Lowry and the staff of Ambassador-Emerald International for their contributions to the publication process and to my husband, Randy, for his patience and enthusiastic support.

Contents

Foreword

The reader may well wonder, "Why a book about saints?" and more particularly, "Why these saints?"

I have been fascinated by the subject of saints since my childhood when I first visited the Museum & Gallery on the campus of Bob Jones University in Greenville, SC. There I saw depictions of St. Lucy with one pair of eyes in her head and another in a dish. I remember a painting of St. Jerome writing a book, a lion at his feet.

In history class I learned of Joan of Arc. At Christmas time, I sang about Good King Wenceslas and Jolly Old St. Nicholas. I wore green on St. Patrick's Day (until I learned that Protestants should wear orange instead of green), and I decorated a shoe box with hearts and flowers for Valentine parties. As a piano major in college I was introduced to Franz Liszt's setting for piano of the legend of St. Francis walking on the waves. Later, in my writing for BJU Press, my research occasionally led me to wise statements by St. Augustine.

Why a book about these saints? Because I think we have all heard enough about saints and their legends to make us at least wonder about them. Perhaps for all our patchy acquaintance with saints' names and legends, however, we really know very little about the people we call saints. Unfortunately, as Sir Max Beerbohm has said, "Ordinary saints grow faint to posterity; whilst quite ordinary sinners pass vividly down the ages." I chose these particular saints because they are all quite prominent in art, music, and literature. At least, I had come across their names often enough to whet my curiosity. As I read about them, I learned that many of them have been widely misrepresented by the very tributes that have been paid them. This book is intended to instruct, to provide biographical information that should in some cases even inspire and edify.

What is a saint? More will be said in Dr. Woehr's scholarly introduction that follows about how the concept of sainthood developed in history, but just now we should differentiate between the biblical concept and the Roman Catholic idea. First Corinthians 1:2 tells us that saints are all those "that are sanctified in Christ Jesus . . . [who] call upon the name of Jesus Christ our Lord." In other words, saints are believers. There is a sense, of course, in which some believers are more saintly than others in that they act more like Christ. As the great Puritan divine Thomas Watson wrote, "A true saint is a divine landscape or picture, where all the rare beauties of Christ are lively portrayed and drawn forth. . . . He hath the same spirit, the same judgment, the same will with Christ." But the Bible gives no warrant for making some Christians second-class citizens of heaven, for although saints are "sanctified in Christ Jesus," all their "righteousnesses are as filthy rags."

Roman Catholicism reserves the term saints for a special class of people who are supposedly holier than the rest. We should recognize, however, that many of the qualities that Roman Catholicism has traditionally admired—self-inflicted punishments, lack of bodily care, devotion to the Virgin Mary or to the pope—have no appeal to Bible-believers and find no basis in Scripture. In the early centuries popular recognition made one a saint, but in the Middle Ages a system of canonization or official approval developed. Today a church court investigates the life of a person whose name is submitted for canonization, and evidence is brought forward to determine if miracles have occurred in response to prayers to that person. Not infrequently the church or town possessing the person's relics will have a strong interest in his canonization.

The practice of saint worship is repulsive to Bible-believing Christians, but that should not hinder us from appreciating those dead heroes of the Faith who have been erroneously labeled as servants of the Romanist system. From all that we can gather, such people seem to be genuine saints in the biblical sense, and I have tried to write a just account of their lives. On the other hand, the majority of the thousands of Roman Catholic saints give no evidence of trusting in Christ alone for their salvation (indeed, some could not because they never existed!), and a number of these have also found their way into this book.

Saints & Non-Saints went to press over twenty years ago. When Ambassador International agreed to rescue it from its permanently-out-of-print state, I had no trouble framing its *raison d'être*: history is never outdated; its lessons are timeless. In fact, the potential for the impact of these biographies on the reader might be greater today than when I first related them. Our society is even more hedonistic and materialistic, even less inclined to give up creature comforts, to make personal sacrifices, and to commit to a cause greater than self, than it was in the mid 1980s. We, as members of this society, would do well to recognize that with great affluence comes the threat of cultural decadence and spiritual impoverishment.

I have found, and I hope my readers will find also, a number of my subjects to be very sympathetic and attractive characters, and the accounts of their lives and struggles make dusty history come alive. Except for the legendary "saints" (whom I call non-saints in this little volume), all of these people had one striking characteristic in common: they all dedicated their lives to the task of knowing God. While some of them, despite their best human efforts, seem not to have found Him, they all served as a rebuke to me by their single-mindedness and self-abnegation. To our shame, it is still as true today as it was in 1600 when Thomas Kedder wrote that:

> *This age thinks better of a gilded fool*
> *Than of a threadbare saint in wisdom's school.*

We all have much to learn by the example of these people.

And Satan trembles when he sees
The weakest saint upon his knees.
−William Cowper (1731-1800) and John Newton (1725-1807),
Olney Hymns

The saints are God's jewels, highly esteemed by and
dear to Him; they are a royal diadem in His hand.
−Matthew Henry (1662-1714)

The way of this world is to praise dead saints
and persecute living ones.
−Nathaniel Howe (1764-1837)

To make a man a saint, it must indeed be by grace:
and whoever doubts this does not know what
a saint is, or a man.
−Blaise Pascal (1623-1662)

A true saint is a divine landscape or picture, where all
the rare beauties of Christ are lively portrayed and
drawn forth. He hath the same spirit, the same judgment, the same will with Christ.
−Thomas Watson (d. 1690)

Introduction
By David Woehr

The people included in this book lived over a period of fourteen hundred years, and the last one died more than four hundred years ago. The modern reader will not truly understand these "saints" without some knowledge of the history of the Church during this period, and especially of the development of the Roman Catholic Church over the centuries. We must not assume that someone in the Church who lived before the Reformation believed all or even very much that the Roman Catholic Church teaches today. Instead we should judge each individual case on its own merits.

The Rise of Roman Catholicism

Roman Catholic historians and apologists have traditionally painted a very attractive picture of their Church—the one, holy, universal Church governed by the successors of St. Peter and faithfully preserving their Christian doctrine and practice from all admixture since the days of the Lord's apostles. The attractiveness of this picture lies in the security it offers. Here is an unbroken physical connection with the apostles. One does not have to wonder which is the true Church. Rather than having to grope around in the dark to discover what the Bible means, one merely has to ask the Church for the proper interpretation. There is a relative security in knowing that by being baptized and by staying in good standing with the Church (not the same as living a righteous life) one will eventually get to heaven after purgatory.

Unfortunately, this view of the Roman Catholic Church has little basis in fact. There is no evidence that Peter was ever bishop of Rome, and even if Matthew 16:18 means he was the head of the apostles, Christ said nothing about transmitting such an office to any successors. The evidence suggests that originally a board of elders governed the church at Rome. At times there have been two or three men claiming to be pope, each anathematizing the others. As for continuity of doctrine, numerous examples exist of popes who condemned the acts and teachings of their predecessors. Rivalries and disputes between theologians and between various religious orders within the Roman Catholic Church perhaps exceed in quantity and vehemence those between Protestant groups that consider themselves separate denominations.

The Roman Catholic Church has differed very widely at different stages of its history. In the earliest period of church history, prior to the eighth century, there was a Catholic ("universal") Church scattered across the Roman Empire, but it had no well-organized hierarchy, and the doctrines of Romanism existed only in seed form. The period of Medieval Latin Catholicism, which lasted from the eighth to the sixteenth century, presents Romanism with all of its doctrines and practices, but still in a diversified state. Superstition and evangelical doctrine might dwell beside each other in relative harmony, even in the same person. The Council of Trent (1545-1563) marks the beginning of the modern period. The council clearly defined Roman Catholicism, condemned the distinctive doctrines of Protestantism, and provided the machinery to enforce its decrees. Trent was followed up in the nineteenth century by the proclamation of Mary's immaculate conception (1854), the *Syllabus of Errors* (1864), and the first Vatican Council (1869-1870), which affirmed the pope's infallibility.

The Papacy. A variety of factors favored the growth of centralized authority in the Roman church between the second and seventh centuries, by which time the modern concept of the papacy had become clearly visible. Rome, the imperial city, was a cosmopolitan center, and the large church there included some wealthy members and consequently attracted talented men to serve as its leaders. It also patterned its administrative system after that of the imperial government, an efficient method, certainly, but one destined inevitably to harden into an inflexible bureaucracy. As time went on, such bishops of Rome as Damasus I (366-384), Innocent I (401-417), Leo I (440-461), and

Gelasius I (492-496) advanced the claims of their powers. They began insisting that other churches obey their decisions, and a body of legends and theories to support their claims was gradually built up. By the pontificate of Gregory I (590-604), who marks the division between the ancient and medieval church, the medieval papacy was fully developed, though it experienced periods of decline and resistance to its authority. The apex of papal power was Innocent III (1198-1216), who claimed the right to rule both church and state and often succeeded in imposing his will on both.

The growth of papal government shows the tendency in Romanism for custom and common usage to become firm law and for the abstract and spiritual to become concrete and physical. It was not good enough for Christ to be the Head of the Church; He had to have a visible representative on earth in the pope. It was not sufficient that the Church scattered across the world be unified in having a common Savior and a common faith; it had to have a physical unity in being submissive to the bishop of Rome and in having doctrines and practices identical to his.

Scripture and Tradition. Serious consequences arose from the application of an emphasis on external authority to the doctrine of Scripture. Roman Catholicism teaches that we know the Bible is a divine revelation because the Church has told us so. But the Bible is not the only source of truth, for the Church claims to be the custodian of unwritten traditions passed down from the apostles themselves. Furthermore, the Church is the only official interpreter of these two parallel sources of truth—Scripture and Tradition. Thus the institutional Church sets itself up as a replacement for the Holy Spirit as the Interpreter of God's Word for the believer, an external authority of the inward spiritual witness.

The various doctrines of Romanism manifest this same gradual development and the same subtle twisting of biblical teachings. For instance, the Bible teaches that one whose heart has been changed will repent of his sins and that we may know the reality of the inward work by the outward change. The Roman Catholic Church developed a complex system of penance whereby a person confesses his sin orally to a priest, who prescribes what the offender must do to demonstrate his penitence and then pronounces formal absolution of the offense. Another example is ceremonial baptism. The New Testament teaches a baptism of the Holy Spirit that makes one a Christian and a water baptism that symbolizes the inward work. In Roman Catholic theology, the symbol came to take the place of the real thing so that one supposedly became a Christian when he was baptized with water, a doctrine known as baptismal regeneration.

The Sacraments. As a formalistic or ritualistic religion, meaning one in which the emphasis is placed on outward activities, the Romanist way of salvation is summed up in its sacramental system. While Protestants generally accept two sacraments, Baptism and the Lord's Supper, the Roman Catholic Church has seven: Baptism, Confirmation, the Eucharist, Penance, Extreme Unction, Holy Orders, and Matrimony. It was not, however, until the twelfth century that these seven received official sanction. While Augustine defined a sacrament as a visible sign of an invisible grace, medieval theologians added the idea that they are channels of grace that actually confer the grace of which they are a symbol. Furthermore, the sacraments were thought to do this *ex opera operato*—that is, they have the power in themselves to convey the grace, and the mere performance of the rite in the prescribed manner produces the effect. The Church then became not the body of believers but a sacramental institution with the power to dispense grace to its communicants. Such a conception of the Church transforms the priest from an undershepherd of the flock and a preacher of the gospel, as the Scripture teaches, into almost a magician with the awesome power in his hands of dispensing salvation.

The biblical way of salvation contrasts sharply with the sacramentalism of Romanism. The Roman Catholic Church insists that five of the seven sacraments (they except matrimony and holy orders) are essential for salvation, while the Bible says simply, "Believe on the Lord Jesus Christ and thou shalt be saved" (Acts 16:31). The sacraments, far from having an inherent magical power to confer grace, are, along with the Word and prayer, the means of strengthening and edifying the believer, and the Holy Spirit communicates grace by the sacraments only to those who appropriate it by faith. The purpose of the sacraments, as the Westminster Confession of Faith summarizes it, is

> To represent Christ and his benefits, and to confirm our interest in him; as also to put a visible difference between those that belong unto the Church, and the rest of the world, and solemnly to engage them to the service of God in Christ, according to his Word. (xxvii.1)

Furthermore, the Church is not an external organization that dispenses grace to communicants; it is the body of believers with Christ as their Head (Col. 1:18). They have no earthly priesthood to perform rites and ceremonies to placate God, for there is a universal priesthood of believers: "Ye . . . are built up a spiritual house, an holy priesthood, to offer up spiritual sacrifices, acceptable to God by Jesus Christ" (I Peter 2:5). Christ has indeed ordained that local assemblies have leaders, which the New Testament calls elders or bishops (literally, "overseers"), but they are not an order of sacrificing priests. They preach, teach, shepherd, lead in public worship, and minister to the people, but because "there is no more offering for sin" (Heb. 10:18) after Christ's "one sacrifice for sins for ever" (Heb. 10:12), we have absolutely no need of a separate order of human priests.

Monasticism. Another important element of Romanism is monasticism, the idea that one can lead a more perfect life by secluding oneself away from normal life. The principle in itself is not evil, for the Christian must be separated from the world in many ways and he needs times of solitude, private worship, and meditation; however, it ignores the Christian duty of practical service for the Church and positive influence in the world. Each of us can be pleasing to God in his own calling. As the poet Cecily R. Hallack has put it,

> Lord of the pots and pipkins, since I have no time to be
> A saint by doing lovely things and vigilling with Thee,
> By watching in the twilight dawn, and storming Heaven's gates,
> Make me a saint by getting meals and washing up the plates!

Monasticism is too often linked with asceticism based on pagan dualism, which is the idea that the flesh is inherently evil and opposed to the spirit, and thus the only way to destroy the evil is to destroy the flesh. The ascetic spirit in monasticism has produced the most repulsive examples of fanaticism and subhuman behavior, such as self-mutilation and torture, extreme filthiness of body glorified as holiness, and pitiful acts of self-denial to make oneself pleasing to God. Christian monasticism (pagan religions such as Buddhism also have monasticism) originated in Egypt in the late third century, its first great exponent being St. Antony (Anthony). It became popular in the West in the fifth century through the influence of Jerome and others. Various men drew up rules to govern the lives of monks, the two most influential ones being those of Basil the Great in the East and Benedict of Nursia in the West. It became common for the monk to take three particular vows when he devoted himself to the monastic life: poverty (he could not own property, though the order as a group could), chastity (i.e., celibacy), and obedience to his superiors. A remarkable characteristic of monasticism has been the tendency of orders to decline in fervency and faithfulness to their original ideals. This meant that new orders were constantly being created (as in the case of Francis of Assisi) and old orders reformed (as in the case of Bernard of Clairvaux). Though many noble men and women have given themselves to the monastic way of life, and monastic groups performed many valuable services during the Middle Ages (e.g., copying of manuscripts, education and preservation of learning, and opening new land to cultivation), monasticism drew thousands out of productive lives and more often than not twisted and warped their personalities.

The "Worship" of the Saints

The position of the saints in the Roman Catholic system is at once a pervasive characteristic and one of the most repelling to the Protestant mind. Protestant devotion everywhere emphasizes that the believer has as immediate access to God in prayer as a child does to his father, and the only Mediator is the crucified Savior, who is God Himself. In contrast, the Roman Catholic is everywhere met with barriers between him and God, whether priests, sacraments, or saints.

Knowledgeable Roman Catholics will adamantly deny that they worship the saints. Their theologians insist that worship (Greek, *latreia*) or adoration belongs to God alone, but veneration (Greek, *douleia*) or honor may properly be given to those designated by the church as saints (Latin, *sanctus*, "Sacred, holy") and hyperveneration (Greek, *hyperdouleia*) should be given to the Virgin Mary. The veneration of saints by Roman Catholics involves mentioning their names in public worship, celebrating special religious festivals in their honor, meditating on their virtues in order to emulate them, and invoking their help. However, although the theologians may have these fine distinctions clear in their minds, the practices of the common people have frequently degenerated into flagrant idolatry that cannot be defended on any Christian basis.

The problems with praying to saints and venerating them are manifold. Besides the clear statement that there is "one mediator between God and men, the man Christ Jesus" (II Tim. 2:5), the Bible prohibits the worship of angels (Col. 2:18; Rev. 19:10; 22:8-9). We know that there are guardian angels (Heb. 1:13-14), but there is no indication that departed believers, be they ever so holy, can fulfill the same function. Furthermore, Romanism cannot adequately explain how a single saint can hear the prayers of multitudes from all over the world at the same time. If he can, then he must be omniscient, which would convict Romanists of being polytheists. If instead it is God who hears these prayers and then informs the saint, why do we need his intercession in the first place?

The "worship" of saints and prayers to them developed in clearly discernible steps because of evident causes. The ancient world was familiar with the concept of a patron: a rich or influential person who could obtain some favor for the commoner. Many occasions called for patrons: seeking an important position or government post, winning a court case, avoiding trouble with the law. The natural thought of converts not completely emancipated from old habits was to suppose that God would answer their prayers more quickly if someone else (Mary, angels, or departed Christians) put in a good word for them. The influence of pagan religion was also clear, for the ancients freely prayed to the dead, and their gods and heroes were largely glorified men who possessed supernatural powers.

The innocent beginnings of "saint worship" lie as far back as the second century in the high esteem in which the Church justly held her martyrs. The church at Smyrna wrote in the record of the death of their pastor Polycarp about 160, "The martyrs we love as they deserve, for their surpassing love to their King and Master, as we wish also to be their companions and fellow disciples" (*Martyrdom of Polycarp*, 17). By the end of the second century it was widely believed that martyrdom was a second baptism that purified from sin and assured one's entrance into heaven, and Tertullian (ca. 160-ca. 220) taught that martyrs passed immediately into the presence of God while other believers had to wait for the resurrection. This position easily gave way to the idea of Origen (ca. 185-ca. 254) and Cyprian (ca. 200-258) that the prayers of martyrs were especially effective for the church on earth. Confessors (those imprisoned and perhaps tortured for their faith but not martyred) also wielded great influence in the Church, and people flocked to them to gain favors and blessings and to have them intercede with the bishops in their behalf.

The fourth century witnessed the real rise in popularity for the practice. With the legalization of Christianity and the cessation of persecution, thousands of partially Christianized pagans entered the churches and brought their pagan practices. The average church had six annual feast days set aside for martyrs of local fame, and some of these gradually attained universal honor along with the apostles, angels, and other biblical characters. With the cessation of persecution the ascetic life became a kind of self-inflicted martyrdom by which one could attain saintship. By the early Middle Ages, every day on the calendar was filled, with more than one saint for each day, and each country and most professions had their patron saints.

Also in the fourth century the veneration of relics became significant. A relic is any part of a saint's body or any article used by a saint, and it was superstitiously believed to retain its miraculous powers. Bones, hair, cloth, splinters of the cross, and even pictures (called icons) are some examples. The zeal of some to obtain relics was so great that fights would break out in a crowd that had gathered around a dying hermit. Devotees built chapels over the graves of saints, and pilgrims soon flocked to them. By the Middle Ages relics were considered necessary to consecrate an altar. The trade in counterfeit relics became immense. For example, the quantity of splinters claimed to be from Christ's cross would have been sufficient to build Noah's Ark, and at the time of the Reformation thirteen different churches claimed to possess the forefinger of John the Baptist.

The theology built up around the saints and their relics was very complex. Supposedly a saint is one who does all that God requires of him and more. He therefore builds up a surplus of merit that is available for others and kept in a type of treasury to be dispensed by the Church when it sees fit. If a Catholic desires to use some of this merit or grace, he must obtain an indulgence from the Church by doing some meritorious act or even by paying a sum of money to the Church. It was this practice that angered Martin Luther so much and set him off on the road to the Reformation.

At first one came to be considered a saint either by martyrdom or popular acclamation. Soon it devolved upon a metropolitan bishop to designate festivals for saints, and finally the pope reserved the right for himself in the tenth century. The process of canonization, or official approval of saints, continued to develop and came to its present form in the sixteenth century. Before a person is canonized, he must first be "beatified," which allows him to be called by the title "Blessed" and to be honored in a limited way. The act of canonization itself is preceded by an investigation of the person in question on the basis of his sanctity and, unless he was a martyr, whether miracles have been performed as a result of prayers to him. A sort of trial takes place with an *Advocatus Diaboli* ("Devil's Advocate") arguing against him and an *Advocatus Dei* ("God's Advocate") defending him. Canonization means that the person is now in heaven and thus presumably able to intercede with God to gain answers for those who pray to him, and the entire Roman church honors him publicly and privately.

The Miracles and Legends of the Saints

Our knowledge of the saints comes from various sources. Those who were historical personages of some importance, such as Augustine and Jerome, often left numerous formal writings, letters, and autobiographical information, which are often supplemented by contemporary biographies. For a great number of the thousands of saints honored by the Greek Orthodox and Roman Catholic churches, however, we must rely on second-hand sources that frequently received written form centuries after the person supposedly lived.

The second-hand sources are as vast as they are untrustworthy. A group of Belgian Jesuits known as the Bollandists labored from the seventeenth to the twentieth centuries sifting through the thousands of manuscripts in which the lives of the saints have been preserved in order to produce critical biographies of them. Called by various names—lives, acts, passions—the confused mass of material that forms our primary source of knowledge about the saints began accumulating in the second and third centuries with individual accounts of martyrdoms like that of Perpetua. When churches began formal celebrations of anniversaries of the deaths of martyrs, they compiled simple lists as church calendars. Out of this concept grew the Roman Martyrology, the official list of the Roman Catholic Church.

In the fourth century Eusebius of Caesarea and Jerome each composed books of short biographies, but their scholarship and reliability were not the norm. With the decline of Roman civilization, superstition and ignorance became common and contributed to the corruption of the traditional stories. People would come up with farfetched explanations for the titles of saints or the symbols they found on their tombs. Exaggeration and embellishment of the details twisted them beyond recognition, and often saints with the same names would be confused.

These legends of the saints abound in fantastic miracles. Their marvels include healings, protection from the axe and fire, moving mountains and diverting rivers by a single word, resurrections from the dead—the list is almost endless. Furthermore, such earthshaking events often occur for trifling reasons or trivial purposes. The observations of B. B. Warfield bear repeating:

> The question asks itself why the saints, many of whom had severe sufferings to undergo, many of whom were life-long invalids, never rescued or healed themselves by the exercise of their miraculous powers? . . . That the Martyr-heroes . . . ultimately succeeded in dying is a standing wonder. They are delivered apparently from every imaginable, and often unimaginable, peril at the cost of every imaginable, and often unimaginable, miracle; fire will not burn them, nor steel cut their flesh; the sea will not drown them, nor will chains bind them. They bear a charmed life and walk unscathed through every conceivable danger. And then suddenly their heads are simply chopped off as if it were the most natural thing in the world—and they are dead.
>
> The reader catches his breath and cannot believe his eyes: the exceeding *sang-froid* with which the author kills at the end those whom nothing can harm in the meantime produces nothing less than an enormous anticlimax. Has the miracle-power of the martyr given suddenly out—been all used up in its wonderful action hitherto? Or is it merely that the invention of the author has been exhausted, and he has to close thus lamely because he can think of nothing else to say? (*Counterfeit Miracles*, p. 251)

In a word, the legends of the saints bear all the marks of mere folk tales, and in fact modern Roman Catholic scholars freely admit that no educated person can believe them, for the most part. For instance, Hippolyte Delehaye (1859-1941), a well-known scholar and president of the Bollandists, wrote a book entitled *The Legends of the Saints* in which he remarks on the clear difference between hagiography (i.e., writings about the saints) and history:

The work of the hagiographer may be historical, but it is not necessarily so. It may take any literary form suited to honouring the saints, from an official record adapted to the needs of the faithful to a highly exuberant poem that has nothing whatever to do with factual reality. (p. 4)

In a similar vein, Donald Attwater, another noted Roman Catholic scholar in the field, tells us,

Of the numerous written accounts of the early martyrs, a small proportion are authentic. Many of the rest were written after all memory of the true story had been lost, and are wholly fictitious; others are a combination of history and legend, and the respective elements cannot always be disentangled easily, or at all. . . . These "legendary Lives" . . . were meant to be taken seriously, but it may be questioned whether they were always meant to be sober history. They have to be judged accordingly. We cannot but reject them as history and marvel that they could ever have been accepted as such. . . . (*The Avenel Dictionary of Saints*, pp. 12-13)

This were all well and good except that many multitudes have believed the stories literally and taken them for proof of the validity of Romanism. We may live in an age of science, but the number of people who rely on astrology demonstrates that most people are as superstitious and as gullible as ever. The devout in the Roman Catholic Church still do believe many of these miracle stories, and they pray to the saints to perform miracles for them today. Furthermore, the Church claims that they still occur, and she makes them the basis of canonization and hence the veneration of the saints that performed the miracles.

The whole question of miracles has become an important one in our day, especially with the rise of the Charismatic Movement and its emphasis on faith healing. No Christian can deny that God performs miracles, but the question is whether He gives power to men today as in the days of the apostles to alter the course of nature on a regular basis. Furthermore, does a miracle in itself confirm that a miracle worker is from God? This latter question finds an easy answer in Deuteronomy 13:2, which forbids us to listen to a prophet who brings false doctrine and "a sign and a wonder." To cite a particularly offensive instance, some of the Catholic mystics who have experienced the phenomenon called "the stigmata" (the sudden appearance of physical wounds identical to those of Christ) insist that they are helping the Savior bear the sins of the world. The miracles performed by Roman Catholics prove no more than the miracles Pharaoh's magicians performed in imitation of Moses.

Though some orthodox Protestants have disagreed in the past, it seems best to interpret the New Testament miracles as authenticating the apostles themselves rather than the Church itself. The conclusion would then be that the miracles passed away when the apostles died. If the purpose had been to prove the divine nature of the Church, there would be no reason that the miracles would not continue today. What, then, of the many reports of miracles in the post-apostolic Church? The answer lies in the distribution and source of these reports. We find few reports before the fourth century, and all (with the alleged exception of Gnostic and apocryphal documents) were second-hand. In the fourth century the miracles increase dramatically, and the reason must lie in the great influx of pagans into the churches who brought with them their heathen folk tales replete with marvelous supernatural events. One may prove this by noticing how often nearly every detail of a Christian miracle story is identical to a pagan story. To quote Warfield once again,

> In one word, what we find, when we cast our eye over the whole body of Christian legends, growing up from the third century down through the Middle Ages, is merely a reproduction, in Christian form, of the motives, and even the very incidents, which already meet us in the legends of heathendom (*Counterfeit Miracles*, p. 83).

Roman Catholicism Today

The reader may well ask how much of what has been described here as the doctrines of the Roman Catholic Church is still believed by Catholics today. A hundred years ago Protestants looked at Roman Catholicism as monolithic and unchanging, for indeed since the Reformation the Roman Church had loudly proclaimed its virtue as an unchanging church. The Protestants agreed that it was as bad as ever. The situation today, however, seems very different.

The Second Vatican Council (1963-1965) inaugurated a new epoch in the history of the Roman Catholic Church. For decades the "fortress mentality" had come under fire from within the Church by those who insisted on some adjustment to the modern world. Some leading Catholic theologians were strongly influenced by "liberal" Protestant views, and they wanted the freedom to pursue the same lines of thought. Finally, Pope John XXIII summoned a council to address the issues, and in his opening speech made the unprecedented assertion that "the substance of the deposit of faith is one thing, and the way in which it is presented is another." In other words, the Church possesses the truth, but it may not have expressed it adequately, which was a subtle way of backing off from a position without seeming to change. What has resulted was not a change in the basic theology, but a shift in posture, emphasis, and spirit.

For example, chapter seven of the Church's statement on the Church reaffirmed its belief in what the Council of Trent has said about purgatory and the saints, which was "that the Saints who reign with Christ offer their prayers to God on behalf of men, that it is good and useful to invoke them in supplication and to have recourse to their prayers, their help and their succour for the obtaining of benefits from God." Vatican II then added, "This Synod urges all concerned to work hard to prevent or correct any abuses, excesses, or defects which may have crept in here and there. . . .The authentic cult of the saints consists not so much in the multiplying of external acts, but rather in the intensity of our active love."

Today the Roman Catholic Church is filled with conflicting voices. The content of its official theology remains the same, however, and the vast majority of Catholics in the world profess their belief in whatever the Church teaches. Since Vatican II a number of trends have altered the situation considerably, especially in America. For one thing, that council sanctioned several reforms that allowed an increased role for the laity in the parish churches, although not all parishes chose to implement them. By itself this would mean little, but when one considers the situation with the priesthood, the status of the laity may be like the proverbial hole in the dike.

Since 1970 Catholicism has had an explosion in membership. Worldwide its adherents have leaped from 653 million to over one billion, while in the U.S. the change was from 45.6 million to 64 million. At the same time the number of clergy has plummeted precipitously, in the U.S. from 58,632 in 1965 to less than 42,000 currently. This means that there are more and more laypeople for each priest. The number of parishes with no resident priest has risen dramatically, and lay ministers frequently fill the gap. Reportedly, this calamitous decrease arises from the priests' desire to marry. On top of this, in 2002 the revelations of widespread sex-abuse by priests and of the complicity of bishops in covering it up created an enormous scandal. The wide publicity it has received in the secular press has shattered the traditional image of the priest as a trustworthy father figure.

All of this adds up to a state of affairs in which a large number of American Catholics feel free to disagree with the Church's teaching and yet consider themselves good Catholics. (This is particularly true in such areas as abortion, contraception, homosexuality, celibacy of the clergy, and the ordination of women, key issues in which the modern secular culture disagrees with Catholicism.) Attracted by the pageantry of the Church's rituals, its involvement in social issues, or the comfort of having a close community of likeminded individuals, average Catholics' knowledge or concern about its theology may be miniscule.

Romanism is an authoritarian religion that will never abdicate its power if it can help it. While the priests have lost a great deal of the control they once wielded over their parishioners, the hierarchy still has absolute authority over the status of both priests and laity. However, lay people provide the money and an increasing amount of the manpower, so they cannot be entirely ignored today. It is hard to say how far the Church will bend its dogma in order to maintain its power and position. Judging by how the hierarchy has responded to calls for change in recent years, one should expect a long and bitter struggle. Roman Catholicism will not return to biblical Christianity, and those evangelicals who have converted to or agreed to cooperate with the Catholic church are sadly deceived by this religion of bondage. This is a reliable observation, even though no one knows what changes are in store for Catholicism.

• • •

The conclusions we should draw from a consideration of the historical context surrounding the ancient and medieval saints have been embodied in the structure of this book. In Part One we see some famous Christians, who, while by no means perfect, deserve our respect and emulation. Often they did not escape from the errors of their age, but their true Christian spirit and devotion to the Lord mark them as real heroes of the Faith. In Part Two are historical personages who were part of the problem, propagators of the characteristic errors of Romanism, bound and deluded by a satanic system. Finally, in Part Three there are the legendary or semi-legendary characters who may have existed but whose stories are so intermingled with the fabulous that little can be known for sure. Yet, like secular legends, their stories are often charming and interesting and have become part and parcel of our culture.

–David Woehr, PhD

Recommended Reading

Boettner, Loraine. *Roman Catholicism*. Philadelphia: Presbyterian and Reformed, 1962.

Brewer, Bartholomew, and Furrell, Alfred W. *Pilgrimage from Rome*. Greenville, S.C.: Bob Jones University Press, 1982.

Hudson, Henry T. *Papal Power: Its Origins and Development*. Welwyn, Hertfordshire, England: Evangelical Press, 1981.

Kerr, William Shaw. *A Handbook on the Papacy*. London: Marshall Morgan and Scott, 1950.

Schaff, Philip. *History of the Christian Church*. 8 vols. 1910; reprint Grand Rapids: Eerdmans, 1972. See especially vol. 3, pp. 409-465; vol. 5, pp.700-763.

Warfield, B. B. *Counterfeit Miracles*. 1918; reprint Edinburgh: Banner of Truth, 1972.

I have devoted this first section to historical figures of the Christian church about whom the record has been relatively generous. Because we possess a good deal of reliable information concerning them, we have little difficulty recognizing what is fact and what is fiction. In most cases, we can listen to the people as they speak for themselves from autobiographies or recorded testimony. Our only problem is to understand them as people of another era.

The biographies included in this section have all been "sainted" by the Roman Catholic Church, but Protestants can object to its taking exclusive possession of them. Perpetua met a martyr's death before the Roman Catholic Church really existed. John Chrysostom and Augustine were fathers of the entire Christian Church, whether Greek, Roman, or Protestant, and they lived at a time when those distinctions did not exist. Patrick was a noble Christian missionary who carried on his work outside the pale of Romanism. Bernard is perhaps a borderline figure, but in a number of areas he rises above the superstitions of the Middle Ages.

Part One

Perpetua
John Chrysostom
Augustine of Hippo
Patrick
Bernard of Clairvaux

Perpetua, Martyr
Of Carthage

Like many stalwart Christians who died for their faith, third-century Perpetua would be surprised to find her name in the calendar of Roman Catholic saints. Unlike many so-called saints whose names are connected to a Roman feast day, Perpetua lives on in history, not in papal legend, but in her own words. Perpetua's record of her life and sufferings just prior to her martyrdom gives us special insight into the testimony of this courageous young woman who served Christ in life and death.

Perpetua's account takes us to Carthage in North Africa in the year A.D. 203. Perpetua was twenty-two years old, from a well-established family, liberally educated, married, and the mother of an infant son. While the account reveals nothing of her husband, we do know that her mother and two brothers were Christians, and that her father remained a pagan.

In the year 202, Emperor Septimus Severus of Rome had issued an edict to persecute Christians. On its authority, Perpetua, four men, and another woman, Felicitas, who was expecting a child shortly, were arrested and imprisoned in a private house.

Perpetua's father visited the house to try to dissuade her from her faith in Christ. "Father, do you see this vessel?" she asked him, pointing to a water pot. "Can it be called by any other name than what it is?"

"No," he replied, whereupon she said, "So also I cannot call myself by any other name than what I am—a Christian."

The Christians were soon transferred from house arrest to prison. Perpetua wrote, "I was greatly frightened because I had never known such darkness. What a day of horror! Terrible heat, owing to the crowds! Rough treatment by the soldiers! To crown all I was tormented with anxiety for my baby!"

Two deacons arranged for the prisoners to be transferred to a better part of the prison, where Perpetua obtained permission to keep her baby with her that she might nurse him. "Being relieved of my trouble and anxiety for him," she wrote, "I at once recovered my health, and my prison suddenly became a palace to me and I would rather have been there than anywhere else."

Perpetua's brother requested that she seek to learn from the Lord whether "suffering or release [were] in store" for her. She answered, "And I, knowing myself to have speech of the Lord for whose sake I was suffering, confidently promised [to bring him word]." That night while she slept she received the assurance that they "must suffer, and henceforth began to have no hope in this world."

When the news reached Perpetua's father that the prisoners were soon to be examined, he again visited Perpetua, hoping to weaken her resolution.

"Daughter, pity my white hairs," he began. "Pity your father. . . . Make me not a reproach to men! Look upon your son who cannot live long after you are gone." The old man wept and kissed her feet as he spoke. Perpetua, much moved, wrote, "And I grieved for my father's sake, because he alone of all my kindred would not have joy at my martyrdom."

The day arrived for their examination, and the prisoners were summoned to the market place. A huge crowd had gathered. The Christians were placed upon a platform facing the procurator of the province, Hilarian. Perpetua recorded the event: "The rest, who were questioned before me, confessed their faith. When it came to my turn, my father appeared with my baby, and drawing me down from the step besought me, 'Have pity on your child.' The procurator Hilarian joined with my father and said, 'Spare your father's white hairs: spare the tender years of your child. Offer a sacrifice for the prosperity of the emperors."

Perpetua refused and boldly affirmed her faith. When her father attempted once again to intercede, Hilarian ordered him to be beaten off. She wrote, "This I felt as much as if I myself had been struck, so greatly did I grieve to see my father thus treated in his old age."

Hilarian then sentenced them all to torture and death by wild beasts in the arena. Perpetua testified that they returned joyfully to their prison to await their execution. Once at the prison, Perpetua asked for her baby, but her father refused to send him. As if to remove her source of anxiety, "God so ordered it that the child no longer required to suckle."

Another blessing of her remaining time in prison was that Pudens, the officer in charge of the prison, "began to show [them] consideration, perceiving that there was some great power within [them]." He allowed frequent visits from Christian friends, which refreshed them in their trials. Later, he too professed Christ.

On the evening before the scheduled games in the arena, Perpetua felt certain of the Lord's sustaining presence. She looked forward to her death, "And I saw that I should not fight with beasts but with the Devil: but I knew the victory to be mine." She added significantly, "I have written this up to the day before the games. Of what was done in the games themselves, let him write who will."

An eyewitness recorded the events of the next day. Felicitas, Perpetua's fellow-prisoner, had feared that she would not be able to suffer with her friends because pregnant women were not allowed to be executed publicly. She and the others prayed that she would give birth early. Accordingly, she delivered a daughter while in prison and committed the baby to Christian friends for adoption. Thus, on March 7, the small band of believers marched together to the arena for their final ordeal. The men went first, followed by Felicitas, "rejoicing to come from the midwife to the gladiator," and Perpetua, "abashing with the high spirit in her eyes the gaze of all."

The men were released to the ferocity of the beasts first. After their first encounter with a bear and a leopard, one of the Christians, Saturus, who was only wounded and was allowed to rest near the spectators, had opportunity to encourage his jailer, Pudens, to be firm in the faith.

Perpetua and Felicitas were exposed to a savage heifer. Perpetua was gored and thrown first, but she sat up immediately, gathered her torn tunic around her and went to the aid of Felicitas. The crowd, amazed by their calm demeanor, shouted that it was enough. The women were taken from the arena for a few minutes. During this respite, Perpetua called to her brother and another young Christian, "Stand fast in the faith and love one another; and do not let our suf-

ferings be a stumbling block to you." When the crowd demanded that
they be brought again into the arena, the women went willingly "after
giving each other the kiss of peace." They were killed by gladiators,
and Perpetua "herself placed the wavering right hand of the youthful
gladiator to her throat," since he had only wounded her in the ribs by
his first stroke.

The story of Perpetua, recorded as it was by one of her contemporaries, had such an impact on the African church for the next two
hundred years that Augustine issued a warning that the document
should not be revered as Scripture. He also mentioned the martyrs
in a sermon prescribing the attitude his listeners should have about
their story:

> It is no small part of imitation to rejoice in the virtues of
> them that are better than we. If we may not follow them
> in deeds, let us follow them in affection; if not in glory, at
> least in gladness; if not in merits, in prayers; if not in their
> passion, in our compassion.

John "Chrysostom"

John Chrysostom enjoys the distinction of being the greatest orator of the Greek church. The surname Chrysostom, meaning "Golden Mouthed," was affixed to his Christian name sometime after his death, and it bears testimony to the beauty and power of the many sermons he preached. His homilies are still widely admired today, although the flowery, effusive style in which they were delivered has long been considered outdated. Something of the godliness, courage, and force of character of the man lives on in the content of those homilies—something that time and fashion cannot invalidate.

John was born about 347 at Antioch in Syria. He described Antioch as the "head and mother of the Eastern cities." His father, Secundus, was a high-ranking Roman military officer who died when John was an infant, leaving his wife a widow at twenty. John had an older sister who apparently did not survive early childhood.

John's spiritual upbringing was due to his mother's conscientious effort. Anthusa was a devout Christian, and in keeping with the beliefs of many church leaders she refused a second marriage. She devoted all her efforts to the proper rearing of her young son, in whom she could already discern unusual ability and spiritual perception.

Recognizing the value of the best possible secular education, Anthusa enrolled her son as a pupil of Libanius, the famous rhetorician of Antioch. A pagan, Libanius nonetheless had the utmost respect for this Christian pupil. In fact, when asked later whom he would wish to succeed him, Libanius responded, "John, if the Christians had not stolen him."

When his training was complete, John chose the practice of law as his profession. He was well equipped for a brilliant career and made a name for himself as an orator. But the vices that sullied the reputations of other barristers repulsed him. Lawyers, according to John, "maintained the dignity of the legal profession by furnishing a rich client with subtleties to confound the plainest truths, and with arguments to cover the most unjustifiable pretensions." To accept payment for lying for a client was to receive the devil's own money, in John's opinion. He felt he must withdraw from the profession if he was to retain his integrity.

Perhaps it is during the next three years that we may date John's conversion. There is no reference to a conversion experience in his sermons and letters, which are our best source of biographical information. At no point during his youth or early manhood was John rebellious, so it may be that his conversion took place even earlier. At any rate, after resigning his duties as a lawyer, John devoted himself to a study of the Scriptures in preparation for his coming baptism. John's baptism was performed by his bishop, Meletius, in 370, when John was twenty-three.

After his baptism, John's first inclination was to forsake the entanglements of the big city by joining a monastic retreat. To his credit, however, he yielded to the tender entreaty of his mother and remained at home:

> My son, my only comfort in the midst of the miseries of this earthly life is to . . . behold in thy traits the faithful image of my beloved husband. . . . I ask only one favor from you: do not make me a widow a second time; wait at least till I die. . . . But as long as I breathe, support me by your presence, and do not draw down upon you the wrath of God by bringing such evils upon me who have given you no offense.

Instead of retreating to the desert, he chose to convert his home into a monastery. He ate simply and little, slept on the floor, maintained virtual silence, and prayed at length. Naturally, his former legal associates ridiculed his unsociable behavior. He had three intimate friends, however, Basil, Maximus, and Theodore, who joined him in seclusion and studied the Scriptures with him under the direction of the theologian Diodorus.

Theodore was engaged to a young lady whom he dearly loved, and after a time, he decided to withdraw from seclusion in order to marry her. Shocked by this decision, which he considered as heinous as apostasy, John wrote two letters entitled "Exhortation to Theodore." In this rhetorical tirade John uses all of the devices of his craft: warnings, gentle pleas, reproaches, and elaborate imagery. He defined the beauty of women as "nothing else but phlegm, and blood, and humor, and bile, and the fluid of masticated food." He suggested that Theodore's soul was in danger if he were to forsake his religious calling: "To sin is human, but to persist in sin is devilish; to fall is not ruinous to the soul, but to remain on the ground is."

Theodore succumbed to the persuasions of his friend, broke his engagement, and continued his monastic life, later to become a bishop and able scholar.

John was a strong adherent of the prevailing views of his day regarding the superiority of celibacy over marriage. The monastic ideal of "marriage only to Christ" had a strong appeal to the young man. Later in his life, he could encourage his congregation to lead normal family lives to the glory of God, but at twenty-eight, he could think of marriage only as an odious millstone around the neck of an aspiring servant of God.

In 374, following the death of Anthusa, John left the city for the mountains south of Antioch, there to lead the life of a monk for the next six years. He dressed in a coat of goatskin and slept on straw. He recorded the program the monks followed. Before sunrise, the men would gather to sing hymns of praise, followed by a time of prayer under the direction of an abbot. After prayer, they studied the Scriptures and then worked the land to provide their daily support. There were other times of prayer at nine, twelve, and three. In the evening, after a good day's work, they assembled for a simple meal of bread and possibly a vegetable. After joining to sing a thanksgiving hymn, they retired for the night. According to John, their lives were free from care or grief. When one of them died, they spoke of his being "perfected," and all desired a similar end.

Even this simple existence did not satisfy John's yearning for absolute self-denial, so for two years he lived by himself as a hermit in a cave. He spent his time in prayer, study, and writing, never allowing himself the rest his body needed. His health broke under these rigors, and he was forced to return to Antioch to recover, since it was not his intention to end his life in seclusion. He felt that he had profited from his time alone that he might carry on a better public ministry.

Immediately after his return to the city in 381, he was ordained a deacon, a position that allowed him to become intimately acquainted with the needs of the people, their illnesses, and various problems. A few years later he was made a presbyter. In this capacity he entered the major work of his life—his preaching ministry.

John became immensely popular. The people of Antioch packed the church to hear him preach. It was not his appearance that attracted them—he is described as short and bald, with hollow cheeks, a short beard, high forehead, and deep-set, piercing eyes. The qualities that won the people were his uncompromising loyalty to Scripture, his eloquence in communicating it, his obvious love and sympathy for individuals, and his almost fanatical holy life.

John was not primarily a theologian. His talents lay in illustrating existing theology for his people to understand and practice. Nor was he primarily concerned with battling the heresies that his contemporaries Jerome and Augustine were fighting. Rather, John's burden was for the large metropolitan area with which he had been entrusted—an area that was nominally Christian but was polluted with the remainders of paganism and with the numerous vices to which great cities are subject.

Regardless of topic, John used the Scriptures as his primary source book. "The Word," he said, "he said, "is spoken indeed to all, and is offered as a general remedy to those who need it; but it is the business of every individual hearer to take what is suited to his complaint. I know not who are sick, I know not who are well, and therefore I use every sort of argument, and introduce remedies suited to all maladies, at one time condemning covetousness, after that touching on luxury, and again on impurity; then composing something in praise of . . . virtues in their turn."

Yet, John was most emphatic that his hearers must not rely solely on his preaching for their understanding of the Scriptures. "Tarry not," he told them, "for another to teach them for thou hast the oracles of God. . . . Take them wholly unto thee; keep them in thy mind. This is the cause of all evils, the not knowing the Scriptures."

As a Bible teacher, John was a proponent of literal exegesis, as opposed to the allegorical exegesis then in vogue. For this reason men still study his sermons. His commentaries and other works, while of uneven merit when examined by today's standards of Bible scholarship, reveal his gift for sound interpretation, based on common sense and the historical setting of the text.

The spectrum of topics with which John dealt in his sermons is too broad to be covered here. We will look at a mere sample.

About soulwinning he said:

> Nothing can be more chilling than the sight of a Christian who makes no effort to save others. . . . To hide our light under pretense of weakness is as great an insult to God as if we were to say that He could not make His sun to shine.

Commenting on John 1:38, he said:

> When we have begun, when we have sent our will before, then God gives us abundant opportunity of salvation. When God sees us eagerly prepare for the contest of virtue, He instantly supplies us with His assistance, lightens our labors, and strengthens the weakness of our nature.

This comment on the relative freedom of the will contrasts with Augustine's sterner theology of grace. On the other hand, he pointed out, "We can do no good thing at all except we be aided from above."

John inveighed long and loudly about the improper use of riches:

> I blame not those who have houses, and lands, and wealth, and servants, but wish them to possess such things in a safe and becoming way. And what is "a becoming way?" As masters, not as slaves; so they rule them, be not ruled by them; that they use, not abuse them. . . . [God] wishes them to be spent, therefore He has permitted us to have them, that we may impart them to each other.

John was capable of using satire and humor. He says mildly about widows, that they "are a class who, both on account of their poverty, their age, and their natural disposition, indulge in unlimited freedom of speech (so I had better call it)." Here he is a diplomat. In other matters, he becomes more blatantly accusatory, as for instance in this sermon, in which he satirizes the craze for silk shoe strings:

> A ship is built, manned with sailors, furnished with pilots, the sails are spread, the sea is crossed, . . .the merchant . . . after countless risks . . . secures these silken strings, that, after all, you may place them in your shoes. So on the earth the eyes are fixed, instead of upon heaven, filled with anxiety as you walk on tiptoe through the Forum lest you

will stain them with mud in winter or cover them with dust
when summer is at hand.

During services when John was especially fiery, bold, or enter-
taining, the people would sometimes break into loud applause. John
attempted to squelch these outbursts:

What need have I of these plaudits, these cheers, and tumul-
tuous signs of approval? The praise I seek is that ye show
forth all I have said in your works. Then am I an enviable
and happy man, not when ye approve, but when ye perform
with all readiness whatsoever ye hear from me.

Ironically, they even applauded when he rebuked them for applauding!

In Antioch, only a year after his ordination as presbyter, John had
opportunity to utilize all of his skills to meet a crisis. The people of
the city, enraged over high taxes, revolted against Emperor Theodosius the Great, broke down statues of him, his dead wife, and two
sons, Arcadius and Honorius, and dragged the fragments through the
streets. The emperor retaliated by threatening to raze the entire city.
Bishop Flavian, under whom John served, departed immediately for
Constantinople to try to appease the emperor's wrath. John, in the
period of intense anxiety that followed, delivered a series of twen-
ty-one sermons, appropriately called "Homilies on the Statues," in
which he comforted the people, offered hope, and appealed to them
to abjure their sins. During this time of calamity, the people began
to fast and show outward signs of repentance, hoping to avert God's
judgment. John's concern was for their souls: "Practice then the real
fasting—not merely an abstinence from meats, but from sins too—for
fasting is of little avail, unless it be accompanied by a fit state of mind.
Fasting is unprofitable except all other duties follow it."

Flavian was not immediately successful in his mission to Constantinople, but his efforts, combined with the pleas of many monks and
hermits, who arrived to intercede for the distressed city, were finally
honored with success, and the city was spared.

In 398 Nectarius, patriarch of Constantinople, died, and a successor was sought. John was the choice, although he did not know of
his "election" to the office until he was spirited away from Antioch
by military escort and transported to Constantinople. The people of
Antioch would have opposed the removal of their beloved preacher
and would perhaps have done so with force, hence the secrecy. Once
in the capital, John, knowing it was pointless to resist, submitted to

ordination at the hands of Theophilus, patriarch of Alexandria, a corrupt ecclesiastic who had hoped to see a pawn of his elected to the lofty position. Since by the Council of 381 the archbishop of Constantinople was accorded authority commensurate with that of the bishop of Rome, the position to which John was elevated was enviable indeed, at least from Theophilus's point of view. He bided his time, waiting for the moment when he could oust John, whom he knew to be a man of integrity who would not serve his purposes.

John, single-minded and unsophisticated in the ways of politics and its intrigues, lost no time putting into effect drastic reforms among the clergy under his jurisdiction. Whereas his predecessor had lived and entertained lavishly, John gave away his large income and lived in ascetic simplicity, as had always been his habit. He made enemies by denouncing the frivolity of both the clerics and the wealthy aristocracy. Unfortunately, he accomplished his reforms without diplomacy or tact. Those whom he criticized thought him irritable and obstinate.

Nonetheless, the people of Constantinople rallied to him as had the people of Antioch. Preaching was once again his means of greatest influence and the reason for his popularity. His zeal extended beyond his church of St. Sophia to the tribes of Goths who had settled in the area of the city and beyond. He was responsible for a significant missionary effort.

John reached a pinnacle of popularity—even the empress Eudoxia participated in his services and praised his preaching extravagantly. But her adoration was only superficial. She resented John's influence over her weak husband, Arcadius, and she aspired to be the virtual power behind the throne. Like Theophilus, she waited until the moment was right for John's overthrow.

Despite the apparent friendship of the court, John did not soften his messages to win their continued favor. He made unguarded remarks about painted Jezebels, which the ladies of the court took to be caricatures of themselves. Thus insulted, Eudoxia was only too happy to help when Theophilus set his plot in motion.

In 401, Theophilus cruelly and forcefully expelled a group of monks from the Egyptian desert, ostensibly because they defended the peculiar teaching of the third-century church father Origen, but more probably because of a dispute over church funds. About fifty monks, including the four leaders known as the "Tall Brethren," sought sanctuary in Constantinople from the persecution. John, while not a sympathizer with the heretical speculations of Origen, appreciated the teacher's merits and felt that the monks had borne an injustice at the hands of Theophilus. He wrote Theophilus to intercede in the monks' behalf, but without success. Theophilus accused John of harboring heretics and interfering in another man's affairs.

The case of the persecuted monks reached the emperor, who commanded that Theophilus travel to Constantinople at once to stand trial before John. But instead of coming as an accused man reporting to a superior, Theophilus arrived with a huge retinue of dependent bishops and a bodyguard, refused the hospitality of John, who had prepared to receive him, and set up headquarters in a suburb of the city. There he convened the notorious "Synod of the Oak," composed of disgruntled clergymen who, with Eudoxia, had felt the sting of John's accusations.

Arcadius urged John to proceed with Theophilus's trial, but John delivered only a few rather conciliatory messages to the treacherous prelate, as if unaware that the man was even then in the process of unseating him.

The thirty-six bishops, meanwhile, drew up a list of false charges against John, among them immorality and high treason. With Eudoxia's help, they succeeded in deposing John and sentencing him to banishment. John refused to answer the preposterous charges before a hostile council. Knowing that one rash word from him could cause an insurrection among members of his loyal congregation, John quietly surrendered himself to the imperial officers and boarded a ship that was to take him to Hieron, a port city on the Black Sea. Before he left, he assembled his heartbroken bishops and encouraged them not to forsake their charge. He emphasized that "the doctrine of Christ did not begin with me; it shall not die with me." His concern was only for the church he left behind.

After his departure, the people surrounded the palace and demanded the return of their bishop. That night there was a great earthquake. Eudoxia, terrified that the city would be judged by God for her duplicity, implored Arcadius to recall John. She wrote John a letter of apology: "Let not your reverence imagine that I was cognizant of what had been done. I am guiltless of thy blood. I remember the baptism of my children at thy hands."

At his return, a convoy of ships was dispatched to meet him. The harbor blazed with torches, and the whole city converged on the shore to welcome the bishop. For two brief months the church at Constantinople enjoyed tranquility, but then once again John found himself the center of controversy.

In September of 404, Eudoxia directed that a porphyry column topped by a silver statue of herself be erected in the square before the church of St. Sophia. The raucous celebrations held in honor of the unveiling disturbed John's services inside the church. John, disgusted at the pagan display, voiced his displeasure in his sermon, reputedly making the dangerous comparison: "Again Herodias rages, again she raves, again she dances; again, she demands the head of John on a charger."

John's criticisms were reported to the empress, who once again supported a council to depose the bishop. New charges were brought, and while the council deliberated, John received an order forbidding him to preside at church functions. John replied, "I received the church from God my Saviour, and am entrusted with the care of the people's souls. I cannot desert. Throw me out by force if you will; then you, and not I, will be responsible for the non-performance of my duties."

At an occasion just before Easter when three thousand catechumens were preparing for baptism in St. Sophia, an officer entered to break up the service. Soldiers rushed into the church, beating the catechumens and driving them half-clothed into the streets. Blood stained the water in the baptistry, and the scene became one of confusion and gross brutality. At another place, to which many of the baptismal candidates had fled, soldiers robbed and insulted the women and dragged many of the congregation to prison.

Five days later, John was formally deposed. Once again he gathered his closest associates and said farewell, this time forever. In a letter written later, he commented:

> Will the empress banish me? Let her banish me. "The earth is the Lord's and the fullness thereof." Will she command that I be cut in pieces? Let me be sawn asunder, for so was served the prophet Isaiah before me. Will she throw me into the sea? I remember this was the fate of Jonas. Or into a fiery furnace? I shall have the three children for my fellow-sufferers. If she will cast me to wild beasts, I shall think how Daniel went the same way to the lions. If she should command that I be stoned, let it be so. I have Stephen the proto-martyr on my side. Will she have my

head? Let her take it; John the Baptist lost his. Has she a
mind to my estate? Let her have it. Naked came I into this
world, and naked shall I go out of it.

John had scarcely left the city when the church was consumed by
fire, and John's friends were accused of setting it. During the rest of
that week, his clergy were pursued, interrogated, and in some cases
tortured. Olympias, a noble deaconess, testified when charged with an
incendiary act, "My life up to this time is an answer to such a charge.
A person who has expended so much on church-building is not likely
to destroy churches."

John, who heard belatedly of the problems besetting his people,
wrote letters of concern and encouragement to them. His correspondence with Olympias is especially notable for the courage and faith
that it reveals him to possess under trying circumstances.

The first place to which John was exiled was Cucusus, a lonely
mountain village remarkable for the severity of its winters, located
in present-day Armenia. John suffered greatly en route to Cucusus,
but once there, recovered, at least for a time, and was able to carry on
a huge correspondence. His letters, 242 of them extant, influenced
the people of the Empire even more than his presence in the capital.
Porphyry, the bishop of Antioch, wrote, "This dead man rules the
living; this exile conquers his conquerors."

Eudoxia, frustrated because the bishop was still not silenced,
ordered that he be moved to an even more disagreeable and remote
spot in the empire. Pityus, a desert region on the eastern end of the
Black Sea, was the chosen site, and guards were sent to convey him
there. They were instructed to show no compassion to the ailing exile
on the trip, which was to be all on foot. In fact, they understood the
royal intimation that the empress would not be angry if something
were to happen to John on the way to Pityus.

Accordingly, John began the painful journey, but he did not complete it. Three months after their departure, John died in a church
where he had stopped to receive communion. His last words were the
famous motto that he had repeated so often during his life: "Glory be
to God for all things. Amen."

He died on September 12, 407 at age sixty, following three years of
exile and over twenty-five years of faithful preaching.

Innocent, bishop of Rome, when he heard of John's death, wrote
a wrathful letter to Arcadius, saying that a martyr's blood had stained

the hands of both the emperor and his wife, and cutting the emperor off from all church fellowship. Meanwhile, Eudoxia had died after a stillbirth. Arcadius himself died before he could make amends.

Nor did Theophilus outlive John by much. He survived just long enough to express publicly his remorse for having conspired against him. The Church demanded that other participants in the crime against John also acknowledge wrongdoing. John was declared innocent, his deposition illegal, and his name added to a list of apostles and martyrs.

Thirty-one years after his death, John's body was moved to Constantinople, where he was already revered as a saint. The young emperor Theodosius II and his sister knelt beside the coffin and prayed for forgiveness for the sins of their parents against the man of God.

Roman Catholics remember him on September 14, his official feast day. Greek Orthodox observe his day on January 30. Interestingly, most people have heard of John Chrysostom only with reference to the so-called *Liturgy of St. Chrysostom*, which was actually older than Chrysostom, though in all likelihood it assumed his name when he used it in Constantinople. "The Prayer of St. John Chrysostom" appears in the Anglican *Book of Common Prayer* and is taken from the Greek liturgy.

Augustine of Hippo

Accounts of Augustine are full of superlatives: Augustine is undoubtedly the most important figure of the early church after the New Testament age; he is probably the most influential thinker of church history, his writings forming a basis not only for Roman Catholic theology, but also for the Protestant Reformation, and occupying a significant place in the history of philosophy; and, fortunately for history, Augustine is one of the best known church personalities, thanks to his autobiographical *Confessions*, his enormous correspondence, and the excellent biography of Possidius, his lifelong friend.

Augustine was born at Tagaste in Roman Numidia (which roughly corresponds to modern Algeria in North Africa) on November 13, 354. His parents were solid Roman citizens. Patricius, his father, was not a wealthy man, though a member of the council and from a class influential in society. A pagan almost until his death, Patricius was intemperate and sensual. His mother, Monica, in contrast to her husband, was reared a Christian. She was well educated, a loving and forgiving wife, despite her husband's frequent infidelities, and above all, a devoted mother to whose influence Augustine would later attribute his conversion to Christianity. She was a strong authority figure in their home; references to her abound in Augustine's *Confessions*.

Augustine had two older siblings, a brother, Navigius, and a sister, whose name has been lost to history. Augustine distinguished himself at an early age by his outstanding achievements in the local elementary school, and his parents were intensely proud of him. He, however, did not remember his early education with any great love, later referring to his teachers as "executioners" and recalling that his parents were only amused when he complained of being flogged at school.

"The one thing I revelled in was play," Augustine wrote, "and for this I was punished by men who after all were doing exactly the same things themselves. But the idling of men is called business; the idling of boys, though exactly like, is punished."

Patricius, eager for his talented boy to continue his schooling, sent him to nearby Madaura under the auspices of Romanianus, a wealthy and powerful noble whose son Licentius was the same age as Augustine. The two youths, then in their early teens, shared a rented lodging and enjoyed considerable liberty from the restrictions of home. Augustine, while eager to explore the attractions of the city, nonetheless managed to make a good record as a scholar. His parents decided to save their money in order that he might finish his studies in Carthage, the capital city two days' journey from Tagaste. For a year, Augustine remained in Tagaste until his father was able to send him to Carthage. That year of idleness was the boy's moral undoing. He wrote of his tempestuous, adolescent passions, "I burned for all the satisfactions of hell. . . . Both love and lust boiled within me, and swept my youthful immaturity over the precipice of evil desires to leave me half drowned in a whirlpool of abominable sins."

As foul as Augustine later recalled his immorality to be, the offense that seemed to pain him the most was an incident of theft. He and some friends robbed a pear tree, not because they wanted the fruit, but out of sheer perversity. This incident, he felt, was an example of the gross depravity of his heart. "The malice of the act was base and I loved it—that is to say I loved my own undoing. I loved the evil in me—not the thing for which I did the evil, simply the evil."

By the time he set out for Carthage, his sensual desires were overpowering and could not be curbed by his mother's concern and moral reminders, which he considered "womanish" and thus to be scorned the more. He wrote, "I was not yet in love, but I was in love with love. . . . I sought some object to love, since I was thus in love with loving. . . . And I did fall in love, simply from wanting to. . . . I was loved, and our love came to the bond of consummation: I wore my chains with bliss but with torment too, for I was scourged with the red hot rods of jealousy, with suspicions and fears and tempers and quarrels."

The object of his love was undoubtedly the unnamed, lower-born girl who bore his son, Adeodatus, in 372 and with whom he lived for the next fifteen years. Their relationship, while not an official marriage, was nonetheless not condemned by Roman society of that era. This type of union was distinguished from formal marriage only by the absence of legal restrictions and the ease with which it could be begun or dissolved.

Augustine, ensconced with a family in Carthage, did not forget his purpose in the capital—to master the study of rhetoric. He absorbed learning and had a voracious appetite for more, but his sin, the recollection of Christian training, and his ever-questioning intellect, caused him internal dissatisfaction. At this period he was introduced to a now lost work by Cicero entitled *Hortensius*, which affected him profoundly and caused him to vow to make the attainment of truth his lifelong quest. He knew instinctively that his mother's religion was likely to bring him to his ideal, yet his pride kept him from accepting her Savior. He had tried to understand the Scriptures, but he declared, "What I came upon was something not grasped by the proud, nor revealed to children. . . . And I was not of the nature to enter into it or bend my neck to follow it. When I first read those Scriptures . . . they seemed to me unworthy compared with the majesty of Cicero."

In this frame of mind, he was an easy target for the Manicheans. This Eastern sect was founded on the teachings of Mani, a Persian born about 216 who considered himself the prophet of Jesus Christ and the promised Paraclete. His teachings, then considered to be a Christian heresy, were actually a completely independent, dualistic religion that originated in the Zoroastrianism of Persia. Presenting good and evil as two kingdoms constantly engaged in warfare, the Manichee viewed salvation as possible to those who allowed the divinity within them to triumph over the evil. This triumph was possible primarily through the attainment of wisdom.

It was this emphasis on wisdom that attracted the nineteen-year-old Augustine. The Manichean answer to his questions concerning the origin of evil also won him. Further, Manichees freely criticized the Bible, particularly the Old Testament, and held self-denial and moral purity in high esteem. Augustine became an eloquent champion of Manicheanism, although he never renounced the material world in order to become one of the Elect or "Perfect Ones," on account of the strong attachment to worldly pleasures that he was unable to break. As a Manichean Hearer (a sort of layman), Augustine was permitted to marry, own property, and had only to fast occasionally.

Having completed his studies at Carthage, Augustine returned to Tagaste to pursue a living as a teacher of rhetoric. His reputation for eloquence preceded him to his hometown, but Monica, grieved by her son's heresy, would not permit him to enter the family home. Augustine, his concubine, and their young son were offered residence with Romanianus, Augustine's patron from earlier years. Monica prayed earnestly for her wayward son and was finally comforted by a dream in which she saw him ultimately restored to faith. A local bishop to whom she went for advice assured her that "the child of so many tears could not be lost." She was to need those assurances, for Augustine held to the Manichean religion for nine years.

Augustine became restless in Tagaste after about a year and sought a wider sphere of influence and experience in Carthage, to which he moved in 375, his widowed mother joining the household there. This period of his life was characterized by ardent study and the publication of his first works on philosophy. During this period, Augustine's adherence to Manicheanism began to relax as he started to doubt its vague and superstitious tenets. He hoped that a discussion with the Manichean leader Faustus of Mileve would alleviate his doubts. Their meeting, which occurred in 382, proved a disappointment. Augustine wrote that "on the topics on which they usually speak [Faustus] could talk more agreeably than the others," yet Faustus could not answer the questions that troubled Augustine. While Augustine did not sever all of his ties with Manicheanism after his meeting with Faustus, he ceased at that point to be an enthusiastic disciple.

Besides being dissatisfied with Manicheanism, Augustine disliked intensely the unruliness of Carthaginian students. Hearing that students in Rome were kept well in check, he determined to go there in spite of his mother's pleas. "She . . . followed me to the water's edge, clinging to me with all her strength in the hope that I would either come home or take her with me." He deceived her, however, and sailed away at night while she was praying for him in a nearby shrine to St. Cyprian. "Thus I lied to my mother, and such a mother; and so got away from her." When she discovered his treachery, she had no recourse but to remain, "praying and weeping."

After a bout with illness, Augustine established himself as a teacher of rhetoric in Rome. He continued to study the Latin classics and to debate with learned men on topics of philosophy. Yet, in spite of his ability to dominate intellectual discussions, Augustine was unsure of his own beliefs. His mind was in turmoil. He desired absolutes. He toyed with Epicureanism and the skepticism of the Academics, and for a time he leaned toward Neo-Platonism. The ideas propounded by the literature in which he immersed himself stimulated his thoughts but left his soul restless and still searching.

The prefect of Rome, Symmachus, impressed by Augustine's oratorical genius, recommended him for a position of professor of rhetoric in Milan. Augustine accepted the appointment since his Roman pupils were not faithful in paying their bills, and changed his residence again about 385. His mother soon joined him there.

In Milan, Augustine could not help hearing of Bishop Ambrose, a prominent Christian leader and a powerful speaker. Monica was delighted when Augustine began to join her at church to hear Ambrose preach, even though his avowed reason for attending the services was to observe the great preacher for the sake of oratory alone. Augustine recorded the impression these early visits made:

> Salvation is far from sinners, of the sort that I then was. Yet little by little I was drawing closer, though I did not yet realize it. . . . Along with the words, which I admired, there also came into my mind the subject matter, to which I attached no importance. I could not separate them. And while I was opening my heart to learn how eloquently he spoke, I came to feel, though only gradually, how truly he spoke.

Ironically, though Augustine was close to accepting the beliefs of Christianity, he was perhaps in a worse moral condition than at any preceding time in his life. Monica, in keeping with Augustine's rising social status, had arranged a formal betrothal between her son and a girl of an excellent family. This engagement made it necessary for Augustine to dismiss his companion of fifteen years. Augustine described the parting: "The woman with whom I was wont to share my bed was torn from my side as an impediment to my marriage. My heart still clung to her, it was pierced and wounded within me, and the wound drew blood from it. She returned to Africa, vowing that she would never know another man, and leaving me with our natural son."

Augustine, however, could not make a similar vow of chastity, not even for the two years that he must wait before his intended bride would be of age. Immediately, he wrote, "I procured another woman, but not, of course, as a wife."

Augustine's health suffered along with his emotional state. Recurring asthmatic attacks weakened him and made it difficult to meet his teaching responsibilities. He had a visit from a fellow countryman during this period of depression, a Christian named Ponticianus, who happened to relate the story of St. Antony, a pious but uneducated hermit of Egypt who is called the founder of Christian monasticism. Ponticianus recounted Antony's holiness and the self-sacrificing quality of his life. Augustine recorded his response to the account:

> Ponticianus told us this story, and as he spoke, You, O Lord, turned me back upon myself. . . You stood me face to face with myself, so that I might see how foul I was, and how deformed and defiled, how covered with stains and sores. . . . You placed me . . . so that I might find out my iniquity and hate it. I knew what it was, but I pretended not to.

After the departure of his guest, Augustine became increasingly more distraught as he contemplated the enormity of the power that sin had over him. His boyhood friend Alypius, who shared his lodging, was surprised at Augustine's intensity when he burst out: "What is the trouble with us? . . . The unlearned rise up and take heaven by storm, and we, with all our erudition but empty of heart, see how we wallow in flesh and blood!"

Augustine rushed into the garden to try to still his soul's disquiet. He knew what he must do to have peace, yet he hesitated. "Those trifles of all trifles, and vanities of vanities, my one-time mistresses, held me back, plucking at my garment of flesh and murmuring softly: 'Are you sending us away?' . . . The strong force of habit said to me: 'Do you think you can live without them?' "

He threw himself under a fig tree and wept for his sin, still unable to make a decision to renounce it forever. He asked himself, "How long shall I go on saying tomorrow and again tomorrow? Why not now, why not have an end to my uncleanness this very hour?"

At that moment he heard a child's voice from a neighbor's house, singing over and over, "Take and read, take and read." He stood up immediately, interpreting the little chant as "a divine command to open my book of Scripture and read the passage at that I should open."

He opened his copy of the Pauline epistles, hoping, as he had heard was Antony's experience, that he would find a passage that would bring him to the point of conversion.

So I . . . opened it and in silence read the passage upon which my eyes first fell: 'Not in rioting and drunkenness, not in chambering and wantonness, not in strife and envying. But put ye on the Lord Jesus Christ, and make not provision for the flesh, to fulfill the lusts thereof." (Romans 13: 13-14)

The Word of God illuminated Augustine's heart at that moment. He wrote, "All the darkness of uncertainty vanished away." Calmly now, he testified to his friend Alypius, and the men hurried into the house to tell Monica the happy news.

With his conversion in the spring of 386, Augustine found his goals and desires completely changed. He broke his engagement, resigned his position, partly because of ill health, and wrote to Ambrose requesting baptism, which was then scheduled for Easter of the following year.

A colleague of Augustine offered him the use of his villa on the outskirts of Milan for the summer. Augustine, in need of rest and solitude, gratefully accepted. A small party, including several of Augustine's students, his son, and Alypius, set up housekeeping at the retreat. Monica managed the household.

Augustine had time for Bible study and for the lengthy discussions with his students and friends that he so enjoyed. Augustine's *Confessions* reveals the progress of his Christian growth during this period immediately following his conversion.

From this period also we have Augustine's comments about his gifted son, Adeodatus, with whom he loved to converse as with a much older man. When they returned to Milan for baptism, Augustine wrote:

We also took with the boy Adeodatus, carnally begotten by me in my sin. You [Lord] had made him well. He was barely fifteen, yet he was more intelligent than many a grave and learned man. In this I am but acknowledging to You Your own gifts . . . and power. . . . to reshape our shapelessness: for I had no part in that boy but the sin. . . . His great intelligence filled me with a kind of awe.

Adeodatus, scheduled to be baptized along with Augustine and Alypius, had only a few more years to live, much to Augustine's grief. However, Augustine was confident of his son's eternal salvation, and Augustine, Alypius, and Adeodatus all received baptism together.

After the occasion of their baptism, the group made plans to return to Africa. They had traveled as far as Ostia on the Tiber when Monica became ill. Augustine recorded a scene of unusually sweet fellowship between himself and his mother prior to her death. They were discussing the delights of their life in Christ when Monica addressed Augustine:

> Son, for my part I no longer find joy in anything in this world. What I am still to do here and why I am here I know not, now that I no longer hope for anything from this world. One thing there was, for which I desired to remain still a little longer in this life, that I should see you an [orthodox] Christian before I died. This God has granted me in superabundance, in that I now see you His servant to the contempt of all worldly happiness. What then am I doing here?

She died shortly afterward at the age of fifty-six. Her son was bereft, "but took joy from her testimony."

Augustine remained in Italy for probably another year, studying and writing. He began his written warfare with the Manicheans during this time and also commenced work on a book about free will, a topic that absorbed him both before and after his conversion.

In 388 Augustine returned to Tagaste, a different man from the proud, restless scholar who had left it years before. Here he and his friends lived quietly, pursuing their studies. Augustine, always a teacher, kept up a voluminous correspondence with friends and former students, answering questions for them about spiritual matters. One piece of correspondence of special note was a work entitled *Of True Religion*, which Augustine wrote to his patron, Romanianus, in order to bring him to Christ. That good object was achieved, and the book, when circulated, brought others to Christ as well.

In 391 Augustine visited the city of Hippo, a small town on the Mediterranean that is today known as Annaba or Bône in northeast Algeria. It was there that he began a ministry that was to last for the next forty years. He entered the church at Hippo one day while Bishop Valerius was publicly lamenting a shortage of presbyters. Some in the crowd recognized the famous Augustine, surrounded him, and dragged him to the front of the church, demanding that he become their presbyter. In those days, when Christian people designated their choice, the candidate had no option but to receive the honor.

Augustine had certainly not sought the position into which he was thrust against his will. He had planned to continue his tranquil life at Tagaste, producing works that he hoped would clarify many points of Christian doctrine. He had renounced his life as an orator, only to face again the responsibility of speaking to and convincing the public. He requested that Valerius allow him to return home for a short time in order to regain his "self-mastery" and to prepare himself for his unexpected vocation. His biographer Possidius wrote, "This glowing light which sought the solitude was thrust upon the candlestick."

Shortly after Augustine's ordination, Valerius, who was aging and in need of help, began relying more and more on Augustine and eventually turned over all of the bishop's duties to him. Augustine not only preached, sometimes several times daily, and oversaw the management of the church; he also was responsible to legislate for the townspeople in civic matters. In addition to his heavy pastoral duties, Augustine continued his literary output and became embroiled in countless debates and religious controversies. He also maintained a clerical school, the first monastic establishment in Africa, patterned after the life of study, meditation, and fellowship that he and his companions enjoyed at Tagaste.

Prior to his becoming bishop of Hippo, Augustine underwent dramatic changes in ideas and life habits. After his conversion, however, his life might best be described as a process of continual and consistent growth. The biography, then, must take on a different character. Rather than follow him year by year, an undertaking that would require several volumes, one must now focus on highlights in his ministry and the more outstanding contributions of his pen.

As bishop of Hippo, Augustine continued to live simply. His meals consisted mainly of vegetables, although he served meat to guests and had no objection to taking wine in moderation. His clothing was also simple. He preferred a long black robe with a cowl, which must have contrasted starkly with his long, prematurely white beard. When members of the church offered him more elegant attire, he sold the garments and contributed the money from the sale to the poor. About clothing he said, "It is no doubt permissible for a bishop with a private fortune to wear costly clothing, but would you want the people to say that I found in the Church the means to dress myself better than I could have done in my father's house? A rich dress is no more appropriate when I carry out my obligation to preach than the worn-out body and white hair you see before you."

A decidedly practical man, Augustine was an able administrator of financial as well as spiritual concerns. On three occasions when the church had no funds to help its own poor, ransom a townsperson captured during a time of invasion, or buy burial plots for fellow Christians, Augustine directed that the church vessels be melted down. "It is better," he said, "to save souls for the Lord than to save gold. The most precious vessels are those which deliver souls from death. The Lord's real treasure lies in the operation of His own precious blood."

As a preacher, Augustine was a huge success. Volumes of his sermons survive for our perusal today. These were either transcribed by listeners or written down by the preacher himself after the delivery. He spoke extemporaneously and without rhetorical artifice, which is surprising considering his training, his mastery of oratorical device, and his genius. His style broke every rule of contemporary homiletical "correctness." He used any legitimate means—common illustration from daily life, verse, the element of surprise, humor—to keep his audience involved and thoughtful during his messages. On one occasion, he even composed what became a popular song in order to refute a local heresy. In that simple, rhymed form, the material was easily learned and remembered by his people.

Augustine loved people, and they in turn loved him. He was often baffled that people would visit Hippo just to hear him preach. "My brothers," he said, "You like to come to hear me, but what is it you like? If it is I, even that is good because I wish you to love me, but I do not wish to be loved for myself. For my part, I love you in Christ, so in your turn love me in Him."

Augustine's sermons were a natural overflowing of a mind saturated with the Word of God. He often prayed, "May Your Scriptures be my chaste delight! May I never fall into error in my reading of them. May I never deceive others by my use of them."

Part of Augustine's contributions to contemporary society was his involvement in religious controversy. The leading Christian authority of his day, Augustine was invited to major church councils to decide on matters of heresy and schism, such as Donatism and Pelagianism, both of which were condemned. Unlike his older contemporary Jerome, Augustine spoke against issues, not individuals, and his opinions, based as they were on sound, biblical exegesis carried authority.

His preaching and fervent activity in the church might not have made such a lasting imprint on succeeding generations had it not been

for his literary output, which represents the preservation of all that he
believed and taught. His doctrinal statements remain central to any
discussion of church dogma. Here are some of his comments about
controversial theological issues:

> Man does not sin because God has predestined it, but be-
> cause God is everywhere and at all time present He sees
> the sin that man commits. Knowing the future, God can-
> not be ignorant of acts His creatures will commit through
> the working of their own wills. Knowledge of the future is
> not constraint of the future. In the human order of things,
> God is not the author of what He foresees.

> All men are bound for damnation because of one man's
> fault. Men are set apart from this condemnation, not by
> their own merits, but through the grace of the Mediator;
> that is, they are justified freely by the blood of the second
> Adam. . . . We must understand that no one is set apart
> from that mass of perdition, which results from the first
> Adam, unless he has the gift which he can only receive by
> the grace of the Saviour. The chosen are chosen by grace,
> not because of their own existing merits; for every merit of
> theirs is the result of grace.

> God never does anything that is not just. Adam sinned,
> and since all mankind was present in the first man, all
> shared in Adam's sin. God owes no one anything, and He
> cannot be accused of injustice. But because He is kind and
> merciful, He chooses among men those certain ones who
> will be saved.

> Since [the saints] will not persevere unless they both *can*
> and *will* . . . their will is so kindled by the Holy Spirit that
> they *can*, just because they *will*, and they *will* because *God
> works in them so to will.*

Not only did he speak boldly on topics that were hotly debated,
such as the preceding, he also clarified widely held doctrines, such as
the incarnation, in terms that the average layman could understand:
Christ "deigned to assume human nature [and] appeared . . . as a true
man. The assuming of our nature was to be also its liberation."

About miracles in the Bible and in Augustine's day, he wrote:

"Our ancestors were drawn to the Christian faith by miracles that
took place before their eyes, but after the Church was founded on earth,

do we have need of further proof of the divinity of Jesus Christ?"

Near the end of his life, Augustine was grieved by news of the sack of Rome, and by the many barbarian invasions that threatened the very existence of his own beloved Africa. Concerned as he surely was for the safety of his own people of Hippo, Augustine was infinitely more concerned about their carnal response to calamity. He had hoped for a resurgence of faith in the times of crisis, but instead, he exclaimed, "You learn that people in Eastern lands are weeping over your misfortunes, and you run to the theaters! As each wave of bad news reaches you, the fever rises and you make every attempt to forget at no matter what cost."

The barbarian invasions also gave rise to one of Augustine's most influential works, *The City of God*. In 410 the Goths under Alaric shocked the world when they sacked Rome, the Eternal City and symbol of imperial civilization. Pagans charged that Christianity was the cause of the downfall of the Roman Empire. From 413 to 426 Augustine labored on a vast, meandering work intended to refute the pagan accusations and describe the Church, "the City of God," in its contrast with "the City of Man," the world system. The first ten books concentrate on answering heathen arguments against Christianity; the last twelve present a sort of history of the two cities, delineating their birth, development, and destinies. Augustine's *City of God* stands as the first monumental attempt to construct a Christian view of history, and it dominated political and historical thinking in Western Europe for a thousand years. Noble in its conception, massive in its execution, and brilliant in its insights, it is at once the most powerful apology for ancient Christianity and the blueprint for the medieval church.

While the Vandals held the city of Hippo under siege, Augustine fell sick, yet he remained alert and mentally as vigorous as at any time in his youth. From his sick bed, he directed that the penitential psalms be placed on the walls of his room, in order that he might make "a general examination of conscience." He died on August 28, 430.

It is significant that the only things he left to the church at Hippo were his books. They are our legacy from him as well. His masterpiece, *The City of God*, and his autobiography, *Confessions*, are as pertinent in our generation as in his. His letters, sermons, and treatises number many hundreds and provide insight into life in the fourth-century church. His *Retractions*, written with much labor at the end of his life, is a complete catalog of his writings with editorial comments about each, restating anything he felt was unclear in order to prevent any of his statements from being misconstrued. Possidius, his friend and biographer, himself compiled a list of Augustine's works and stated that he thought no man could possibly read them all. He added, "Yet I think that those who gained most from him were those who had been able actually to see and hear him as he spoke in church, and most of all, those who had some contact with the quality of his life among men."

One can hardly overstate the extent of Augustine's influence on the history of theology, at least for the West. He put the capstone on the ancient formulation of Trinitarian doctrine and the gravestone on the remains of the ancient heresies of Manicheanism, Arianism, and Pelagianism (though, of course, their ghosts still seem to haunt us). Both the Roman Catholic and Protestant communions claim him as their ancestor. On the one hand, the Roman Catholic system took up his emphasis on the unity of the Church as a visible, episcopal organization and his view of baptismal regeneration. On the other hand, both the Lutheran and Reformed churches incorporated into their theology his teachings on sin and grace. These same teachings gave rise to the Jansenist movement in seventeenth-century Catholicism. His writings have formed a starting point for the theological and philosophical discussion of each subject he addressed. Although many men have been more learned than he was, as for instance his contemporary Jerome, yet his wisdom and theological insight rank him among the three or four greatest theologians in church history.

Patrick

"I am greatly a debtor to God, who has bestowed His grace so largely upon me, that multitudes were born again to God through me. The Irish, who had never had the knowledge of God and worshipped only idols and unclean things, have lately become the people of the Lord, and are called sons of God."

This simple testimony by Patrick, the "Apostle of Ireland," differs greatly from the popular conception of "Saint Patrick," whose memory is celebrated by Roman Catholics in "the wearing of the green" on March 17 every year. Legend and folklore would have us believe that Patrick was a venerable Roman Catholic saint, that he was responsible for driving all of the snakes out of Ireland, and that he was a white-bearded, miracle-working, spell-casting magician. In short, the myths surrounding Patrick are as rich and varied as lively Irish imaginations can paint them.

The "real" Patrick was certainly a saint, in the sense that all believers in Jesus Christ are saints. He was not an emissary of the bishop of Rome (the papacy did not then exist), nor was he ever officially canonized by the Roman Catholic Church. He probably would not take credit for ridding Ireland of any snakes, unless one were referring to "that old serpent, called the Devil and Satan" (Revelation 12:9). And the only miracles with which Patrick may be positively associated are the miracles of new birth and changed lives that were evident in literally thousands of his converts in fifth-century Ireland.

Patrick is best introduced to us through his own writings, two of which exist as our only legitimate records of his life and ministry. At the time of his death, his exploits were already becoming fictionalized. During the Middle Ages, "biographies" based on the St. Patrick legends abounded, and these are wholly unreliable. Those interested to-day in learning more of the first missionary to Ireland study Patrick's own writings: his *Confession* and his *Letter to Coroticus*.

The *Confession*, composed near the end of his life, is more a history of the working of God's providence in using Patrick to evangelize Ireland than an intimate personal account. It is not intended to be an autobiography, although it provides many autobiographical details. A "confessor" in Patrick's day was one who had risked his life by follow-ing the Lord Jesus openly. The *Letter to Coroticus* provides insight into Patrick's character and missionary zeal.

Patrick begins his *Confession* with "I, Patrick, a sinner, the rudest and the least of all the faithful, and the most inconsiderable among many," and goes on with a brief description of his parentage. His father was Calpurnius, a deacon, and his grandfather, Potitus, a presbyter. Patrick speaks of the church offices without revealing any consciousness what-soever of the Romanist doctrine of clerical celibacy, a point that Roman Catholic biographers are careful to ignore. The author gives as his place of birth Banavem of Tabernia, which cannot be positively identified geographically today, but which was undeniably somewhere in Roman Britain. His father, in addition to holding the office of deacon, was a *decurion* (a member of the city council).

Patrick's birth date is another matter of conjecture, but authorities concluded that it was sometime around 389. During this era, Britons considered themselves solidly under Roman rule, but in actuality Rome was steadily decreasing her control over the territory. Wars against invaders on the continent claimed all of the Roman military forces that had previously maintained order and provided protection for the citizens of Roman Britain. Thus Britain, and in particular the coastal section of the island, was left defenseless against bands of Irish raiders who swept in from the sea to pillage farms, slaughter townspeople, and carry away slaves.

Banavem was the unfortunate scene of one such raid. Patrick tells us that he was sixteen when he and a great many others were taken captive to Ireland. This calamity he refers to in the *Confession* as "our deservings; for we had gone away from God and had not kept His commandments, and were not obedient to our pastors, who admon-ished us of our salvation."

As a slave, Patrick was put to work tending cattle for his Irish mas-ter. Through these circumstances, Patrick testifies, "the Lord opened to me a sense of my unbelief, that I might . . . be converted with all my heart unto the Lord my God, who had looked upon my humility, and had compassion on my youth and ignorance." Following his conversion, Patrick became a man of prayer. "More and more," he says, "the love and fear of God burned, and my faith increased and my spirit was enlarged, so that I said a hundred prayers in a day, and nearly as many at night. . . for then I felt that the spirit was fervent within me."

After six years in captivity, Patrick records that on a certain night the Lord revealed to him that soon he was to return to his own country and that his ship was ready. When he arrived at the ship and applied for passage, the captain indignantly refused him. As Patrick left the ship he began praying, and before he had completed his prayer, one of the sailors cried after him to return and join the company. After a voyage of three days, they reached land and traveled by foot for four weeks, by which time they had totally exhausted their supply of food. The captain of the ship approached Patrick and said, "What, Christian, do you say? Is your God great and omnipotent? Why, therefore, are you not able to pray for us, that we should not be endangered by famine?" Patrick's reply demonstrates his faith that the Lord would vindicate Himself through this test of Patrick's power in prayer. "Be converted to . . . the Lord our God," Patrick admonished the captain, "for nothing is impossible with him, so that food may be sent to you this day."

Soon the seamen came upon a herd of swine, many of which they slaughtered for food. "Being well refreshed," Patrick continues, "they remained there two nights. . . . After this, the highest thanks were given to God, and I was honored in their eyes."

Patrick's narrative alludes to yet another period of captivity, this one only two months, after which he was finally able to return to his country and his parents' home. "My parents," he says, "entreated me, that after so many years of tribulation through which I had passed, that I never again would go away from them."

However, God called Patrick to return voluntarily to the people who had held him captive a short time before. He saw in a "vision of the night . . . a man coming, as if out of Ireland, with a very great number of letters, and gave one of them to me. . . . When I had read the principal of the letter, I thought that at that very moment I heard the voice of those who lived near the woods of Flocut, which is near the Western Sea. And thus they cried out, as with one voice: 'We entreat you, holy youth, that you come here and walk among us.'"

Patrick commenced his work in Ireland when he was about forty-three. Ireland, in the middle of the fifth century, was almost wholly unevangelized. There is some evidence of a few scattered Christian communities prior to the time of Patrick's arrival, but no lasting work had been established. The Romans, with their state religion, had never invaded Irish territory. The Irish were organized by tribes, each having its own chieftain or king. Their religion was known as druidism, and their priests were called druids. The druids practiced sorcery and performed ceremonies at night in the oak groves, cutting the sacred mistletoe with a golden knife and then sacrificing two white bulls, according to the ancient writer Pliny.

No one can state confidently how many years passed before Patrick answered the call to missionary service in Ireland, whether he went under the auspices of any local assembly, or how he passed the interval of several years between his return from captivity and going back to Ireland. We may assume that during that time period he prepared himself for his future ministry by extensive study of the word of God, for he was very familiar with the Latin Bible, and by some sort of church association, for his *Confession* reveals him to have been a deacon and later a bishop.

Roman Catholic authors speculate that Patrick spent these years studying in a monastery in Gaul and that he was ordained for his mission to Ireland by Celestine, bishop of Rome. But there is no reference at all in Patrick's writings of his having been a monk or of his having received a commission from the Roman bishop. Moreover, it is clear that Patrick received no formal ecclesiastical training. He laments his "rusticity" repeatedly, grieves that he had not availed himself of a better education in his youth, and demonstrates in his writings that his knowledge of Latin was only rudimentary. Scholars point out that the simplicity and straightforward style of Patrick's writings distinguish them from the works of any other early church personality, most of whom had had formal training in rhetoric and ecclesiastical Latin. Patrick's *Confession* and *Letter* reveal that the source of his learning was the Word of God. His narrative is so interwoven with quotations from Scripture that one cannot escape the conclusion that he had absorbed great portions of the Bible.

While Patrick does not enlighten the modern reader with regard to his official church connections, he repeatedly expresses his confidence that his commission to evangelize Ireland came from God Himself.

"God directing me, he says in section XV of the *Confession*, "I agreed or consented with no one in coming to Ireland." In fact, his going to Ireland was opposed, not only by his family, but also by churchmen who apparently doubted that his training was adequate for the job, and by one unnamed man who brought up some sin committed by Patrick while an unconverted youth. Patrick testifies that he remained unmoved in his determination to follow God's call to Ireland. "Therefore," he concludes after narrating the account of the opposition he faced, "I give thanks unto him, who has comforted me on all occasions, so that nothing has hindered me from the accomplishment of that which I had laid down to do, and also of my work, which I had learned of Christ. But rather on account of it, I have felt myself strengthened not a little, and my faith has been proved before God and man."

Details of Patrick's long ministry among the Irish are missing from his *Confession*, but he does provide for us the general outline of his work. We know first of all that he was motivated by a sincere love for the souls of men. More than once he refers to "care and a great anxiety for the salvation of others," and to himself as a fisher of men. "It very much becomes us," he states, "to stretch our nets, that we may take for God a copious and crowded multitude; that wherever the clergy are they may baptize and exhort the needy and willing people."

Patrick does not present himself as a flawless, selfless missionary. He alludes to some of the same problems that any Christian servant in an isolated field faces. He speaks of yearning to see his brethren at home, but tells of his refusal to succumb to homesickness in order that he should not "lose the labor which [he had] begun." He says he had long ago decided that "if I went [to minister to the Irish], I should be with them the residue of my life."

He refers also to his constant battle against the weaknesses of his flesh: "I do not confide in myself as long as I am in this body. . . . The flesh is inimical and always draws to death." But he can add triumphantly at the end of his life, "I am not ashamed in his sight, because I lie not; from the time I knew him, from my youth, the love of God, and his fear, have increased in me, until now, by the help of God I have kept the faith."

Patrick's *Confession* refers to his personal chastity and also to vows that several of his converts took to remain unmarried. This is a peculiarity of his ministry, and not of his alone, as we know from reading of Christians of his age. The "monks and virgins of Christ" to which Patrick refers in the *Confession* may have denied themselves rich food or marriage, but they lived in society as other Christians.

Although Patrick saw much fruit for his labors among the Irish—he refers to the "thousands" whom he baptized—his ministry was not without opposition. Once, he records, "minor kings . . . even desired to kill me, but the time had not come; everything which they found with us they seized at once, and bound myself with fetters; but on the fourteenth day the Lord delivered me out of their power, and whatsoever was ours, was returned to us."

The *Letter to Coroticus* speaks of intense persecution of Patrick and many other believers. The *Letter* is addressed to Coroticus, a British chieftain, whose soldiers had attacked a large assembly of newly baptized believers, killing some and abducting others to sell into slavery. Patrick is strong in his denunciation of the outrage committed against God's people. He holds the chieftain responsible for the crimes his men perpetrated by telling him, "Not only they that do evil are worthy to be condemned, but they also that consent to them."

Although Patrick preaches a powerful sermon of judgment to Coroticus and his men, the tone of his letter is one of compassion and concern for his flock. When he introduces himself to Coroticus, he says that he writes, not because he wished "to utter anything so hard and harsh; but I am forced by the zeal for God; and the truth of Christ has wrung it from me, out of love for my neighbors and sons for whom I gave up my country."

An ancient hymn is also attributed to Patrick and said to have been written when the noble missionary was seeking to convert Leogaire, the most important leader of the island. Philip Schaff, from whose church history the following translation is reprinted, says of it, "It contains the principal doctrines of orthodox Christianity, with a dread of magical influences of aged women and blacksmiths, such as still prevails in some parts of Ireland, but without an invocation of Mary and the saints, such as we might expect from the Patrick of tradition and in a composition intended as a breastplate or corselet against spiritual foes." Here are stanzas five through eleven:

> I bind to myself today,--
> The Power of God to guide me,
> The Might of God to uphold me,
> The Wisdom of God to teach me,

The Eye of God to watch over me,
The Ear of God to hear me,
The Word of God to give me speech,
The Hand of God to protect me,
The Way of God to protect me,
The Shield of God to shelter me,
The Host of God to defend me,
  Against the snares of demons,
  Against the temptations of vices,
  Against the lusts of nature,
  Against every man who meditates injury to me.
    Whether far or near,
    With few or with many.

I have set around me all these powers,
Against every hostile savage power,
Directed against my body and my soul,
Against the incantations of false prophets,
Against the black laws of heathenism,
Against the false laws of heresy,
Against the deceits of idolatry,
Against the spells of women, and smiths, and druids,
Against all knowledge which blinds the souls of man.

Christ protect me today
Against poison, against burning,
Against drowning, against wound,
That I may receive abundant reward.

Christ with me, Christ before me,
Christ behind me, Christ within me,
Christ beneath me, Christ above me,
Christ at my right, Christ at my left,
Christ in the fort [i.e., at home],
Christ in the chariot-seat [traveling by land],
Christ in the poop [traveling by water].

Christ in the heart of every man who thinks of me,
Christ in the mouth of every man who speaks to me,
Christ in every eye that sees me,
Christ in every ear that hears me.

I bind myself today
The strong power of an invocation of the Trinity,
The faith of the Trinity in Unity,
The Creator of [the elements].

Salvation is of the Lord,
Salvation is of the Lord,
Salvation is of Christ;
May thy salvation, O Lord, be ever with us.

Historians have dated Patrick's death on March 17 sometime between 461 and 493, most modern scholars favoring a year very close to the former date. He is said to be buried at Downpatrick in Northern Ireland. His influence has certainly been felt throughout the centuries following his death, although that influence has not always been consistent with historical fact. Patrick, always humble and eager to acknowledge the power of God working through him, concluded his *Confession* with these works: "The gift of God is to be most assuredly credited for what has been done."

Bernard of Clairvaux

Bernard of Clairvaux wielded such a powerful influence over the thinking of his day that the first half of the twelfth century has been referred to as the age of Bernard. Bernard is said to have "carried the twelfth century on his shoulders, and he did not carry it without suffering."

To understand Bernard, one must understand a little of the era in which he lived. The period of the Middle Ages was one of great contrasts—between violent passions and strict asceticism, between grandeur and dismal poverty, between ignorance and scholasticism, and between superstition and enlightened religion. European society was organized under the system known as feudalism, in which vassals held land by contract from higher lords in return for military service and most people were serfs who worked the land. The Church rather than the state was the central power.

It is important to remember that before the Reformation the Church was catholic in the sense that it was universal. The features of organization, ritual, and doctrine that distinguish the Roman Catholic Church of recent history were in the formative stage in the twelfth century. For instance, the Roman doctrine of transubstantiation was not defined until the Fourth Lateran Council in 1215. The Mass was not dominant in Roman Catholic ritual until 1311. The number of sacraments had not been fixed at seven until late in the twelfth century, and the doctrine of the Immaculate Conception was not then an article of faith. As late as 1250 an English bishop could declare with impunity that if a pope were to do something in defiance of Scripture, believers who obeyed him would be disobedient to God, their higher authority.

Bernard's era was notable for its spirit of inquiry. It is known as the dawn of scholasticism, the age in which universities came into being and an interest in learning enjoyed a revival. With study, men became inquisitive, and their questions led to reform in society and in the Church. Bernard was the most prominent among these reformers.

Bernard was born in 1090 near Dijon, France, into the family of Tescelin Sorrel and his wife, Aleth. Tescelin, whose surname describes his ruddy complexion, was renowned locally as a valiant knight and a man of integrity. His wife, from one of Burgundy's noblest families, intended to be a nun, but instead married Tescelin, to whom she bore six sons and one daughter. She remained very devout, dividing her time between household tasks and caring for the needs of the poor in her community.

During Bernard's childhood, while his brothers were involved in military exercises, Bernard was set apart for special study. After his elementary education at home, he was sent to a secular school with the canons (staff members of a cathedral) of St. Vorles at Chatillon, fifty miles away. His progress and aptitude for learning were extraordinary. He began to feel that perhaps he should spend his life in literary pursuits.

When he was seventeen, his mother died. Her death was a shock and a great loss, for Bernard and she had been close, and she had been a constant source of spiritual help to him. It was perhaps because of her influence that Bernard announced his decision to forsake worldly pursuits and enter the monastery of Citeaux, a newly founded and inadequately funded Cistercian house located in a swampy, unhealthful site near Dijon and noted for the severity of its discipline.

Bernard's choice of Citeaux surprised friends and family members. If he must enter a monastery, they argued, why could he not go to a house of Cluny that would be more comfortable and a more appropriate atmosphere for his talents? Bernard replied, "I chose Citeaux in preference to Cluny not because I was not aware that the life [at Cluny] was excellent and lawful but because . . . I am conscious that my weak character needed a strong medicine."

Bernard, who possessed exceptional good looks, wit, charm, and intelligence, could have employed his natural gifts in any number of secular vocations. He sought instead the sort of life he felt would bring him closer to knowledge of God. Nor was he content to embark on his career alone. He enlisted his brothers and several friends to accompany him. In all, he persuaded thirty-one men to join him at Citeaux. They arrived in 1112 or 1113.

Life at Citeaux was difficult by any standards, but especially trying for high-spirited young nobles accustomed to comfort and social activity. At Citeaux the novices were introduced to a regimen of solitude and study. In addition, they raised and harvested their own grain for food. The men had visitors frequently; oftener, in fact, than Bernard would have wished. He found the necessity to converse a distraction, later writing to a novice from his own experience, "I advise you, my son, to avoid as far as you can idle talking with guests."

One of the monks' tasks in the monastery was to correct the text of the Latin Vulgate into which errors had crept over several centuries of use. To this effort and years of subsequent study, historians attribute Bernard's formidable command of Scripture. Butler's *Lives of the Saints* says that "he had so meditated on the Holy Scriptures that in almost every sentence he borrows something from their language, and diffuses the marrow of the sacred text with which his own heart was filled."

In 1115, Bernard, then only twenty-five, had so distinguished himself by his dedication and potential for leadership that Stephen, abbot of Citeaux, sent him with twelve others to start a daughter house about seventy miles away. The men chose a site known as the Valley of Absinthe for the herb that grew plentifully there. Later, the name was changed to Clairvaux, "valley of light."

The site was ideal—there was adequate timber and a good water supply—but while the building was underway, the men had to scrounge for wild berries to eat. While Bernard welcomed the hardships as a challenge, several of the men were becoming discouraged. Two of his brothers, Guy and Gerard, appealed to Bernard in behalf of the other men, some of whom were becoming ill, and suggested they return to Citeaux. Bernard insisted that all that was lacking was faith to believe God would supply their needs. Each time the men faced certain starvation, Bernard would go to prayer, and someone would arrive with a gift of money or food for the new monastery.

Nonetheless, Bernard took his brothers' plea to heart and became more sensitive to his men's physical needs and limitations. As he matured, he looked after his monks with great tenderness and paternal affection. He wrote to the father of one young monk, "Do not worry about the frail health of your son, for I shall look after him like a father

. . . and I will so temper and arrange all things for him that his soul may profit without his body suffering."

Unfortunately, young Bernard did not care for his own health as carefully. He suffered all of his adult life from an acute gastric condition, attributable no doubt to the poor diet and austerities of his youth.

Clairvaux soon won wide renown because of the godly lives of its abbot and monks, and as a consequence the Cistercian movement grew rapidly. Daughter houses were started from Clairvaux, not only in France, but in several other countries as well. But Clairvaux was not without antagonists. The Black Monks (so called because of their black garments) of Cluny, a long-established Benedictine house, resented the growing popularity of the Cistericans, or White Monks of Clairvaux. Because the two houses were in the same district and because their ways of life differed substantially, the two groups were bound to come into conflict.

The Black Monks had developed their own traditions and rituals and conducted themselves with stately grandeur. The Cistercians, on the other hand, deplored ritual and led a life of obvious poverty and withdrawal from the world. Neither group was without its hypocrites, as the leaders of both rival houses were quick to point out. The abbot of Cluny, Peter the Venerable, remained a close friend of Bernard despite the controversy that marked the inception of the Cistercian movement. The two abbots corresponded frequently on the subject of their differences. Peter lamented in one letter to Bernard, "The Black Monk looks down his nose when he sees a White Monk, and a White Monk turns his back when he sees a Black Monk coming."

When Bernard established Clairvaux, he expected to spend his life in his rustic retreat, studying, preaching, and writing. He was well suited for a life of contemplation—his powers of concentration were phenomenal. It is said that once he rode all day on the shores of Lake Geneva without once noticing. On another occasion, he set out on the back of a magnificent and elegantly fitted horse to visit a monastery. His arrival on the animal excited the curiosity of all of the monks, but none was more surprised than Bernard himself. He had borrowed the animal for the trip without really looking at it.

But Bernard was never oblivious to the needs or flaws of the men in his care. His sermons illustrate his keen perception of human nature, and his wonderful capacity for understanding and humor. In one sermon he satirized picky eaters:

> What does it profit a monk to restrain himself from pleasures if he is always bothering about the appearance of his food and how it is served? Vegetables, he says, give me wind, cheese weighs down my stomach, milk is bad for my head, my chest suffers if I drink water, beans make me melancholy, leeks heat my blood, fish from ponds and muddy water spoil my complexion. O I beg you have pity on your own peace of mind and on those who wait on you; try not to burden the house and consider a little the good of your soul.

On another occasion he addressed a sleepy congregation with these words:

> The long Vigils last night excuse your yawns, but what am I to say to those who slept at the Vigils and are sleeping now?

Bernard's writings reveal him to have been of exceptional learning and great devotion to the Word of God. He was known to contemporaries as "the man of love" because of his sincere desire to love God and his fellow man perfectly. His writings on the love of God are still read widely today. The following is an excerpt from his famous letter on the love of God:

> At first a man loves himself for his own sake. . . . When he sees that he cannot subsist of himself, then he begins by faith to seek and love God as necessary to himself. And so in the second stage he loves God, not yet for God's sake, but for his own sake. However, when . . . he begins to meditate, read, pray, and obey, he [begins] to know God and consequently to delight in him. When he has tasted and found how sweet is the Lord, he passes to the third stage wherein he loves God for God's sake and not for his own.

His writings also reveal to the modern reader a great deal concerning the state of church doctrine in his century. Bernard, unlike modern Roman Catholics, looked primarily to the Bible for his theology, not to tradition. About Bible study, Bernard wrote, "Instruction makes men learned; affection [toward the truth] makes them wise. . . . It is one thing to know many riches, another thing to possess them; and it is possession, not knowledge, which makes one rich."

Bernard believed that while the sacraments were among the vehicles of God's grace, assurance of salvation was not built on these, but on faith in Christ. He wrote, "If thou believest that thy sins cannot be abolished except by Him against whom alone thou hast sinned, and upon whom sin cannot fall, thou doest well; but add to it also that thou shalt believe this, that thy sins have been forgiven thee through Him. This is the testimony which the Holy Spirit utters in thy heart." This type of thinking is quite foreign to Roman Catholic theology as it was developing even before the time of Bernard.

He denied that baptism was essential for entrance into heaven, citing the example of the thief on the cross who was not baptized and to whom the Lord promised eternal life in heaven. Bernard also denied that the presence of Christ during the Lord's Supper was something magical. Rather, he insisted, the Lord's presence was to be "appreciated by the heart."

Yet another concept against which Bernard protested was the Immaculate Conception of Mary. Bernard held that Christ alone was conceived without sin, though Mary was sanctified before birth. To say that Mary also was immaculately conceived was to Bernard highly illogical, and that if it were true, sinlessness would have to be extended to all of her ancestors as well. On the other hand, Bernard erroneously saw Mary as a mediatrix between the believer and Christ, and he enjoined those who feared to go to the Father and the Son to pray to her, though he did not approve of worshipping her, and his comments about her are more moderate than those of many of his contemporaries.

Among his writings are four fine hymns that are among the favorites of many Christians: "Jesus, the Very Thought of Thee"; "O Sacred Head, Now Wounded"; "O Jesus, King Most Wonderful!"; and "Jesus, Thou Joy of Loving Hearts." (The reader will find these reproduced at the end of this chapter.) The texts are presented in beautiful, scriptural language that exalts the Lord Jesus and acknowledges the believer's dependence on His merits.

During his first years at Clairvaux, Bernard may have enjoyed the peace and solitude he had sought, but it was not long before his reputation as an authority on biblical interpretation or church policy lost for him his privacy and brought him endless commissions to preach or to mediate disputes. His authority was recognized by kings and popes, who appealed to him for assistance in church and even political matters.

Bernard, though a truly humble man, was absolutely forthright and fearless when dealing with the mighty of his day. His confidence lay not in his own powers, which were nonetheless formidable, but in his God, on whose behalf he sought to act. Once he wrote to a duke who was preparing to fight a count: "If you set out to invade his territory . . . and shed human blood . . . you will seriously anger Him who is 'the Father of the orphan and gives the widow redress.'" . . . If you will not heed the voice of God warning you through me for the good of your soul, then He be your Judge."

Nor did he mince words with the pope. He wrote to Eugenius III: [By your recent actions] "you prove that you have a plenitude of power, but peradventure not so much of justice."

Yet, Bernard, who had a sharp wit, never used it to insult, but rather to persuade. Even those whom he opposed respected his sense of fairness. His were never attacks on a person, but rather attacks on issues.

The disputes Bernard was called on to settle were so numerous that he complained that his life was "over-run in all quarters with anxieties, suspicions, cares, and there is scarcely an hour that is left free from the crowd of discordant applicants, from the trouble and care of business. . . . They do not leave me even time to pray."

In 1130 the news reached Bernard that two popes were claiming supremacy: Gregory Papareschi, who took the name Innocent II; and Peter Leon, who took the name Anacletus II. Vastly oversimplified, the problem was this: Gregory had been elected in a somewhat irregular fashion, since only a minority of the cardinals was present. Peter's supporters, instead of contesting the election, held their own and declared him pope. Anacletus, whose reputation according to contemporaries was not safe even among his friends, then proceeded to take Rome by force and remained armed against any opposition by Innocent.

Bernard, who knew the character of both men, did not hesitate to render his judgment that the first election was the valid one and that Innocent was the true pope. However, eight years elapsed before the schism was healed. Bernard traveled widely, persuading kings and emperors to support Innocent. He presided eloquently at peace councils and continually mediated in local schisms until the death of Anacletus.

In 1141 Bernard responded to another challenge, this one a public debate with Peter Abelard. Abelard was a brilliant teacher with a wide following, but his delight in challenging accepted ideas and his constant attacks on rivals caused his career to be far from peaceful. Bernard had for a long time been alarmed by reports of the man's teachings and was repulsed by Abelard's pomposity. It was inevitable that the two men should come to verbal blows, for they represented two diametrically opposed schools of thought. Bernard emphasized divine revelation and the certainty of faith, while Abelard urged the use of logic and dialectic in searching for knowledge and truth. The two men also differed concerning the doctrines of inspiration, original sin, and the Trinity. While Abelard never openly attacked the church's positions on matters of doctrine, he asserted that one need not accept that which he could not understand or explain. To Bernard, this was a blatant attack on the great mysteries of the faith. He wrote of Abelard:

> He lifts his head to heaven, examines the lofty things of God, and returns to report to us the ineffable words which it were not lawful for a man to utter; and while he is ready to render a reason for all things, even for those which are above reason, he is presuming against both reason and faith; since what can be more contrary to reason than to undertake to transcend it by itself? Abelard defines faith as opinion . . . as if one were at liberty to think and to say whatever he pleases about matters of faith, as if . . . our faith were suspended uncertainly on vague and various human opinions, and were not rather established on certain truth.

The debate was to be held at Sens in June of 1141 and was to be attended by the king of France and a host of church officials, schoolmasters, and others among the country's intelligentsia. Bernard had at first declined the invitation to debate. "I deemed it an unseemly action to bring the faith into the arena of controversy, resting as it does on sure and immutable truth." Abelard, however, had "spread it about on all sides . . . and I was not able to hide myself." Bernard feared that if he refused, his "absence would serve only to increase the influence of the man [and] that his errors might appear to be confirmed if there were no one to answer and refute them." Bernard recorded that he went to Sens "unprepared and unprotected except by those words . . . 'Take no thought of how and what to speak: for it will be given to you in that hour what to speak.' "

Bernard was to open the debate with a reading of collated passages from Abelard's writings. He had scarcely begun when, to everyone's surprise, Abelard interrupted the reading, refused to debate, and appealed instead to Rome. He then left the room.

The reading continued in Abelard's absence. A discussion followed in which fourteen of seventeen passages were condemned. A recommendation to the pope was then forwarded to Rome. As a result, Abelard's writings were formally denounced and the man himself sentenced to a monastery of his choosing, where he died a few years later. His influence was effectively squelched with the Council of Sens. His refusal to participate in the debate seems strange, unless he felt that the pope might be more sympathetic than the council.

The last major entanglement of Bernard's busy life was the Second Crusade, which received its impetus from the news of the fall of Edessa to the Turks in 1144. With Edessa in Turkish hands, Jerusalem's position was precarious. Europeans in general considered Jerusalem the spiritual home of every Christian, and it was not difficult to suggest to them that they must do something to save the endangered city. Pope Eugenius III commissioned Bernard to preach a crusade.

Bernard traveled from town to town in France, gathering huge crowds and stirring their emotions with his message: God, he declared, "has pity on this generation and on those who have grievously fallen away. . . . Look, sinners, at the depths of His pity, and take courage. When almighty God so treats murderers, thieves, adulterers, perjurers, and such like as persons able to find righteousness in His service, what is it but an act of exquisite courtesy all God's own?"

After a few months of preaching, Bernard wrote to Eugenius, "You have ordered and I have obeyed, and your authority has made my obedience fruitful. Towns and castles are emptied. One may scarcely find one man among seven women. . . ." The pope's mandate extended only to France, but Bernard's enthusiasm for the project took him through Germany also, with similar success.

The mission of the crusades was to convert or kill: "We utterly forbid that for any reason whatsoever a truce should be made with these peoples, until such a time as, by God's help, they shall either be converted or wiped out."

In May of 1147, one hundred thousand men left Germany. In June, the king of France departed with his massive forces. By July of 1148 it was obvious that the Second Crusade was an utter failure. The armies were routed, and Bernard was blamed. He wrote to the pope:

> Now the heathen are saying, "Where is their God?" and no wonder, for our armies have perished in the desert or by the sword or from starvation; our princes have quarreled, and fear, misery, and confusion have seeped into their kingdoms. I promised peace and there has been no peace. . . . We know [God's] judgments are true, but this judgment of His is exceeding difficult.
>
> Yet it is nothing to me that I should be blamed. . . . It were better that men should grumble against me than against God.

There were several reasons for the failure of the Second Crusade. One was the complete ignorance of Bernard and others in the West of the true situation in Byzantium. Another was the hostility between the Germans and the French, and still another, the lack of agreement between leaders concerning the best strategy to follow. Further, the enormous size of the armies made it virtually impossible to ensure effective training and discipline, especially considering that many of the recruits were the "undesirables" of Europe.

Bernard returned brokenhearted to his monastery, his remaining few years saddened by the recollection of that fiasco and also by the deaths of several lifelong friends. Near the end of his final illness, he wrote to a friend, "Pray our Saviour . . . that He may watch over my passing . . . so that the enemy who lies in wait for me may find no place where he can grip me with his teeth and wound me." He died surrounded by friends at Clairvaux on August 20, 1153.

The Church of Rome canonized him in 1174. Many histories of his life abounded thereafter, and they are full of accounts of his miracles, supposedly seen by eyewitnesses. These eyewitnesses were young monks who virtually worshiped Bernard and were no doubt eager to ascribe supernatural acts to him. Bernard is said to have restored the power of speech to a mute in order for the man to make a confession of his sins before death. He is also supposed to have had amazing powers of healing, curing the sick by making the sign of the cross over them.

In art his emblems are a pen, bees, or the instruments of the crucifixion. The pen speaks of his writing, the bees of his honeyed eloquence (he is called the Mellifluous Doctor), and the crucifixion instruments of his adoration of Christ as seen in "O Sacred Head, Now Wounded." He has no connection with the breed of dog known as the St. Bernard, which is named after Bernard of Menthon (922-1008), who founded hospices in the Alps.

Hymns by Bernard

"Jesus, the Very Thought of Thee"
(Translated by Edward Caswall, 1814-1878)

Jesus, the very thought of Thee
With sweetness fills my breast;
But sweeter far Thy face to see,
And in Thy presence rest.

Nor voice can sing, nor heart can frame,
Nor can the memory find
A sweeter sound than Thy blest name,
O Saviour of mankind!

O Hope of every contrite heart,
O Joy of all the meek,
To those who fall, how kind Thou art!
How good to those who seek!
But what to those who find? Ah! This
Nor tongue nor pen can show,
The love of Jesus, what it is
None but His loved ones know.

"O Sacred Head, Now Wounded"
(Translated from the Latin into German by Paul Gerhardt, 1607-1676, and from Gerhardt's German into English by James Waddell Alexander, 1804-1859)

O sacred Head, now wounded,
With grief and shame weighed down;
Now scornfully surrounded
With thorns, Thine only crown;

O sacred Head, what glory,
What bliss till now was Thine!
Yet, though despised and gory,
I joy to call Thee mine.

What Thou, my Lord, hast suffered
Was all for sinners' gain,
Mine, mine was the transgression,
But Thine the deadly pain.
Lo, here I fall, my Saviour!
'Tis I deserve Thy place;
Look on me with Thy favor,
Vouchsafe to me Thy grace.

What language shall I borrow
To thank Thee, dearest Friend,
For this Thy dying sorrow,
Thy pity without end?
O make me Thine forever;
And should I fainting be,
Lord, let me never, never
Outlive my love to Thee.

"O Jesus, King Most Wonderful!"
(Translated by Edward Caswall, 1814-1878)

O Jesus, King most wonderful!
Thou Conqueror renowned!
Thou Sweetness most ineffable,
In Whom all joys are found!
When once Thou visitest the heart,
When truth begins to shine,
Then earthly vanities depart,
Then kindles love divine.

O Jesus! Light of all below,
Thou Fount of life and fire!
Surpassing all the joys we know,
All that we can desire.

Thy wondrous mercies are untold,
Through each returning day;
Thy love exceeds a thousandfold,
Whatever we can say.

Thee may our tongues forever bless;
Thee may we love alone;
And ever in our lives express
The image of Thine Own.

"Jesus, Thou Joy of Loving Hearts"
(Translated by Ray Palmer, 1808-1887)

Jesus, Thou Joy of loving hearts,
Thou Fount of life, Thou Light of men,
From the best bliss that earth imparts,
We turn unfilled to Thee again.

Thy truth unchanged hath ever stood;
Thou savest those that on Thee call;
To them that seek Thee, Thou are good,
To them that find Thee, all in all.

We taste Thee, O Thou living Bread,
And long to feast upon Thee still;
We drink of Thee, the Fountain-head
And thirst our souls from Thee to fill.

Our restless spirits yearn for Thee,
Where'er our changeful lot is cast;
Glad, when Thy gracious smile we see,
Blest, when our faith can hold Thee fast.

O Jesus, ever with us stay,
Make all our moments calm and bright;
Chase the dark night of sin away,
Shed o'er the world Thy holy light.

This second section, like the first one, contains historical figures of the Church about whom much is known, but with this difference: our knowledge of them depends heavily on Roman Catholic sources that have freely added to or subtracted from the facts. Thus, when we read of Francis of Assisi, we possess a wealth of undisputed fact along with a ponderous weight of legend. This is less true of Jerome than of the others. There is also another difference: we have little evidence that these people had a personal relationship with Christ as Savior. They were certainly religious, but they seem to have trusted in their own works or a human organization for their eternal destiny. So many of the characteristic errors of Romanism were present in Jerome that in spite of his early date he seems far from true Christianity. The character of Francis is extremely attractive and his humble spirit a rebuke to us all, but he too never disagreed with the Roman Church on the important issues. The reader will have little reason to question that Joan of Arc and Teresa of Avila belong in this category of purely Romanist saints.

Part Two

Jerome
Francis of Assisi
Joan of Arc
Teresa of Avila

Jerome

Jerome, whose full name in Greek is Eusebius Hieronymous Sophronius, was born between 331 and 342 in the town of Stridon, Dalmatia, which corresponds roughly to modern Yugoslavia. Both parents had embraced Christianity, the religion of Emperor Constantine the Great, and they reared young Jerome in Christian principles.

Jerome's father, Eusebius, was well-to-do and thus able to provide his son with the finest education. His early training took place in the public elementary school of Stridon, where he learned to read and write, to memorize and recite, and to do simple arithmetic. There are few clues to his youthful character and the circumstances surrounding his upbringing. In later life he alluded to his boyhood experience when he had to be dragged to school by force, torn from the arms of his grandmother, to whom he was very close. He also recalled being under the care of foster nurses and racing through the slave quarters. Like most boys, he loved food, and looked forward to school holidays.

Jerome showed such unusual aptitude in school that his father decided to send him to Rome to further his education under the tutelage of the famous grammarian Aelius Donatus. Jerome and his boyhood friend Bonosus left for Rome in their early teens. Under Donatus, the boys studied pagan literary classics, rhetoric, logic, some philosophy, and mastered Latin and Greek. It was during this stage of his life that Jerome began building the formidable library that was his lifelong passion. He copied many books by hand, or secured the services of amanuenses (scribes) at great expense.

Removed from the Christian atmosphere of his boyhood home, Jerome was tainted by impurity during his years in Rome. Some thirty years later, he lamented that he had been "befouled with the squalor of every kind of sin" while traveling "the slippery path of youth."

Nonetheless, he never entirely forsook his religious training. He continued his studies as a catechumen (applicant for church membership) and also testified that "it was my custom on Sundays to visit . . . the tombs of the martyrs and apostles."

Around 360 Jerome seems to have experienced a religious awakening. Although he gives no details, we can hope his conversion was genuine. Concerning the doctrine of salvation he said, "It is for us to make a beginning: it is for God to bring it to fulfillment. It is for God to call: it is for us to believe. It is for us to will, or to refuse: but this ability is only ours by God's mercy."

At Treves, Jerome's activities included transcribing works by Hilary of Poitiers, a Latin theologian, for his friend Rufinus. Throughout these years, Jerome transcribed or translated many theological works, thus providing himself with the tools he would later need for his enormous output of commentaries and translations of the Scriptures.

Here also Jerome first became acquainted with asceticism, a system of self-denial and seclusion from worldly influences that was gaining a widespread following in reaction to the superficial Christianity currently fashionable. He felt himself powerfully drawn to accept the demands of monasticism, which became for him the ideal Christian life.

About 370 Jerome moved to Aquileia, near his home of Stridon, and settled there with other ascetic aspirants, among them Rufinus and Jovinian, later to be his opponents in bitter controversy. At Acquileia he met dedicated Christians from all over the western church who were attracted by the teachings of Bishop Valerian.

By this time Jerome had already demonstrated his pugnacious attitude toward all who differed with him. He became an outspoken apologist for all traditional positions of the Church. His wide literary education equipped him to argue his points with eloquence and formal logic. These, supported by his keen wit and genius for biting satire, won for him many admirers, but also many enemies.

In 372 an unnamed quarrel broke up the group of friends. Jerome traveled to Palestine, reaching Antioch in 374 along with three companions. Two of them became ill and died, and Jerome himself nearly died of fever. While delirious one night, he had a dream in which he saw himself standing before the judgment seat of Christ. Asked for his identity, Jerome replied that he was a Christian. "Thou liest," the Judge replied. "Thou art a Ciceronian: for where thy treasure is, there is thy heart also." Jerome then swore, "Lord, if ever again I possess worldly books, if ever I read them, I shall have denied You."

Jerome took the dream so seriously that for many years he refused to read the pagan classics, although he could not bring himself to destroy his library. As an old man, he moderated his views about literature and used examples from the classics in his writings and teachings. Rufinus at that time accused Jerome of breaking his vow. Jerome replied that while the dream had made a great impression on him, he did not feel bound to any promise made in a state of delirium: "Yes, I confess it, I often dream. How often have I dreamed that I saw myself dead and laid in my grave. How often have I seemed to fly above the earth and cross mountains and seas in my flight. Am I then obliged to live no longer? Or ought I, at your demand, to fix feathers on my shoulders . . . ?"

His dream and his meeting with the hermit Malchus convinced him of the benefits of ascetic seclusion in order to immerse oneself in Scripture. He therefore purposed to withdraw to the wilderness of Chalcis.

In that "wild and stony desert" he occupied a cave for four years, living alone and eking out a meager existence for himself from unfruitful soil. There were communities of anchorites (that is, monks who lived as hermits) nearby with whom he met frequently for worship. He surrounded himself, even in these most primitive conditions, with theological books and copies of the Scriptures.

Despite the penance and self-mortifications he practiced, he was tormented by severe temptations of the flesh. He wrote that while "burnt up with the heat of the scorching sun . . . , I seemed to be in the midst of the delights and crowds of Rome . . . witnessing the dancing of the Roman maidens. . . . My face was pallid with fasting, yet my will felt the assaults of desire."

To conquer his temptations and regain victory over the flesh, Jerome determined to learn Hebrew. "When my soul was on fire with bad thoughts, as a last resort I became a scholar to a monk who had been a Jew, to learn of him the Hebrew alphabet."

Often he despaired of mastering the language, with its "hissing and broken-winded words," but master it he did, more fully than any scholar of his day, and that mastery enabled him to translate the Old

Testament from the original language, a pioneer effort in the fourth-century Latin church.

Jerome had never yet found the peace he had sought in his travels, and he was not to find it in the desert either, despite his retirement from society. Against his will he was drawn into a dispute among the desert monks concerning the doctrine of the Trinity. They wished him to speak authoritatively on the issue. He refused, referring the matter to Damasus, bishop of Rome, to whom he wrote twice for the official pronouncement of the Roman See.

Jerome, whose writings were earning him the reputation of a learned churchman, became disenchanted with his life in the desert. He was disillusioned by the pettiness and inconsistencies of fellow monks. On leaving the desert, he resided in Antioch with his friend Evagrius and was ordained a presbyter, somewhat against his wishes. He still felt himself called to a life of asceticism and did not care to exercise his priestly functions.

From Antioch, a city torn by religious controversy, Jerome went to Constantinople, there to enjoy a period of pleasant association and study under the devout Gregory of Nazianzus. During his three-year stay in Constantinople, he studied theologians such as Origen and did extensive translations of their works.

In 382 Jerome left Constantinople to attend a council in Rome called by Damasus to deal with the continuing schism in Antioch. Jerome took an active role in the discussions and was soon appointed ecclesiastical secretary to Damasus. Such was Jerome's influence with the bishop of Rome that he could assert, "Damasus was my mouthpiece." At his suggestion, Jerome undertook a revision of the Gospels in the Latin Bible because they contained the inaccuracies of inept correctors and careless scribes.

In addition to his work as a Bible scholar, Jerome became the spiritual guide to a group of prominent Roman ladies who desired to adopt an ascetic way of life. Their withdrawal from the excesses of Roman society caused a veritable uproar among pagans and some professing Christians.

At first Jerome enjoyed the esteem of nearly all of Rome for his personal holiness and great learning, so much so that he was considered a possible successor to Damasus, who had become the subject of vile gossip. Jerome was criticized, though, by churchmen for his efforts to correct the errors of the Latin Bible and was vilified endlessly for his association with the noble women Marcella and Paula and their daughters.

Always outspoken, Jerome did not seek to endear himself to his accusers. He called the churchmen "two-legged asses" who preferred to drink "of their muddy rivulets, rather than of his waves of a more pure spring."

He published damaging satires in the form of letters to the chaste women under his direction. In these he lashed out at fashionable Christian women who

> Paint their cheeks . . . and eyelids . . .: whose plastered faces, too white for those of human beings, look like idols, and if in a moment of forgetfulness they shed a tear, it makes a furrow where it rolls down the painted cheek; they to whom years do not bring the gravity of age, who load their heads with other people's hair, enamel a lost youth upon the wrinkles of age, and affect a maidenly timidity in the midst of a troop of grandchildren.

In 384, with the death of his patron, Damasus, Jerome found himself the center of scandal, particularly concerning his relationship with Paula. He prepared to leave Rome and seek a new beginning in the Holy Land. He embarked late in the summer of 385. In his letter of parting to the Lady Asella, he wrote in his own defense, "Salute Paula and Eustochium, mine in Christ, whether the world will or no . . .; and say to them, we shall stand before the judgment seat of Christ, where it shall be seen in what spirit each has lived."

In Antioch nine months later Jerome was joined by Paula and her daughter, Eustochium, as well as other Roman women of every class who desired to found a monastic retreat for women in the Holy Land. Jerome, with his brother Paulinian, who was many years his junior, and several monks, began a tour of biblical sites in the company of the Roman women. Jerome made extensive notes of their travels and recorded his observations of existing monasteries in the east.

In 386 the group settled in Bethlehem, where Paula expended some of her ample fortune to build a double monastery—one for monks and the other for her nuns, and also a hospice for pilgrims, "so that," in Paula's words, "should Mary and Joseph again visit Bethlehem there would be a place for them to lodge in."

Finally Jerome enjoyed for a time the peace that he had long sought. Despite his busy schedule of directing the monastery and the guest house, he was able to continue his translation work, his commentaries on books of the Bible, and his extensive correspondence with other church leaders. He was often asked to answer questions regarding the meaning of certain Scriptures.

A friend who visited Jerome in Bethlehem commented, "He was constantly immersed in study and in books; continually occupied in reading and writing, he permitted himself no rest day or night."

Jerome did not record a great deal concerning the operation of his monastery. In a letter to Rufinus he provides this clue: "Always find some work to do, never let the devil find you idle. . . . Weave baskets of need. . . . Hoe the soil and plot your garden."

About Paula's nunnery we have more complete information: the women were divided into three groups according to social class and had separate living quarters. They assembled at dawn, nine, noon, sunset, and midnight for prayers and singing. The rest of their time was devoted to reading and memorizing Scripture and to maintaining the monastery. The three groups of nuns assembled together on Sunday for worship.

In many different letters, Jerome outlined his expectations for holy women. They were to deny themselves rich food, beautiful garments, the luxury of bathing and careful grooming, and frivolous company, taking for their companions only those who were "given to fastings, whose face is pale." They were to devote themselves to the study of the Bible: "Let sleep overtake you in the midst of your studies, and the sacred Scriptures pillow your drooping head."

Jerome described his surroundings in these idealistic terms. "Here bread and vegetables grown with our own hands, and milk, country fare, afford us plain and healthy food. In summer the trees give us shade. In autumn the air is cool and the fallen leaves restful. In spring our psalmody is sweeter for the singing of the birds. We do not lack wood when winter snow and cold are upon us. Let Rome keep its crowds, let its arenas run with blood, . . . and . . . the senate of ladies receive their daily visits."

But Jerome, even in his retreat, could not remain silent when controversy threatened what he perceived to be Christian truth. From his monastery he clashed swords verbally with such men as Jovinian, John of Jerusalem, Rufinus (by this time a leader of monks in Palestine), Vigilantius, Augustine of Hippo, and Pelagius, a contemporary teacher later declared a heretic.

Jerome wrote to Augustine once, "I have never spared heretics; I have spent all my zeal in making the enemies of the church my own." Regrettably, Jerome was not content to deal just with an issue or heresy; he attacked the men themselves, resorting to coarse language and unbridled abuse. Even more unfortunate, because he was overly sensitive to criticism, he often made quarrels where there need not have been any. While he had an intimate acquaintance with Scripture and wrote numerous commentaries, he was not above ignoring the plain meaning of the text when it contradicted his cherished views, especially regarding monasticism and asceticism. And when it came to controversy, he often relied on rhetorical devices such as exaggeration, personal abuse, and bombast rather than valid evidence, sound logic, and fair exegesis.

Of particular interest to Protestants are the views of Jovinian and Vigilantius, who might be considered Reformers before their time. Jovinian questioned the perpetual virginity of Mary, a church tradition that Jerome upheld, and suggested that Mary had other children by Joseph after Christ's birth. Vigilantius questioned the superiority of celibacy and the monastic state and objected to the veneration of relics, calling those who adored ashes and bones idolaters.

On the question of Mary's perpetual virginity, Jerome was vehement. After all, the matter of promoting chastity, along with the translation of the Hebrew Bible, had consumed his energies since his youth. He believed that virginity was vastly superior to the married state, and thus it was necessary that Mary be considered a virgin, even after bearing Jesus. To suggest that she would have been the wife of Joseph in the physical sense was to Jerome a hideous blasphemy.

Jerome asserted that the commands to "multiply and replenish the earth" were not applicable to his dispensation. Jerome did not "deny that wives and widows may be . . . holy women; but it is they who cease to be wives; who in [marriage] imitate the chastity of virgins." He further states that the one redeeming feature of bearing children was that of dedicating those offspring to a life of chastity. Marriage, according to Jerome, replenishes the earth; virginity peoples heaven.

Jerome defended monasticism by saying that monks must fly from temptation because they recognize their own weaknesses.

About the veneration of relics, Jerome said, "We do not worship the relics of the martyrs; but we honour them that we may worship Him whose martyrs they are." He suggested that it is appropriate to pray to dead apostles and martyrs: "If [they] while still living . . . can pray for other men, how much more may they do it after their victories. Have they less power now they are with Jesus Christ?"

A controversy in which Jerome stands in a very poor light is that surrounding the third-century theologian Origen. Origen (185-254), who lived in Alexandria and then Palestine, was the most learned and industrious Christian scholar of the first three centuries and the first to devise a comprehensive system of theology. He wrote so many commentaries on Scripture and works of theology and apologetics that Jerome said he wrote more than other men read. However, Origen was led into certain errors by his attempt to present Christianity in terms of Platonic philosophy. He spiritualized the future resurrection, alleged the existence and fall into sin of human souls before history began, and taught that all men and fallen angels (even the devil) would be ultimately restored to fellowship with God. In fairness to Origen, one should remember, as Philip Schaff wrote, that Origen "propounded his views always with modesty and sincere conviction of their agreement with Scripture, and that in a time when the church doctrine was as yet very indefinite in many points." As a pioneer he made his share of mistakes.

Certainly no orthodox writer could endorse Origen's theology without qualification, but that was no reason to condemn him completely either. In the controversy, which arose about 395, both extremes were taken. Jerome, who had always admired Origen without adhering to his "heresies," took an official stance in opposition to him. Rufinus, who in actuality shared Jerome's appreciation for only the acceptable points of Origen's theology, refused to be cowed by the accusations and chose to come out in support of Origen. As part of his defense, Rufinus undertook a translation of Origen's works, editing freely where he felt he could improve on the master's orthodoxy. In his preface to the work, Rufinus implied that Jerome was an unqualified adherent to Origenism. Jerome, who received a copy of the damaging preface before its intended publication, was outraged.

Thus ensued a regrettable battle between the one-time friends, notable for the vehemence of the attacks each made on the other's character, and for the scandal the argument caused in Christendom. The rift was never healed. When Rufinus died in 410, Jerome described the event as the death of a scorpion.

Fortunately, the controversy with Augustine of Hippo, whom Jerome never met, was conducted in a friendly, even affectionate, manner through correspondence. The fact that the debate never degenerated into mud-slinging was due largely to Augustine's marvelous tact. Their correspondence dealt mainly with the matter of Paul's censure of Peter in the second chapter of Galatians. Jerome, typically, supported the traditional church view—that the two apostles had staged the disagreement to provide an object lesson for the church. Augustine, on the other hand, preferred to explain the passage as it appeared at face value, without the deception that the traditional view implied.

In 404, fifty-six-year-old Paula died, an event that shattered Jerome and caused him temporarily to put aside his works of scholarship. Within a few years, Rome was sacked by the barbarian invader Alaric, and Bethlehem became a refuge for hundreds of refugees. Jerome willingly assisted the homeless Romans who arrive at his hospice. "I have put aside . . . almost all study. For today we must translate the words of the Scriptures into deeds, and instead of speaking saintly words we must act them."

Once again, at the end of his life, his work was interrupted, this time by a mob of Pelagian supporters who set fire to the monasteries, killed one monk, beat others, and sent all of the occupants fleeing for their lives to find sanctuary where they might.

Jerome died on September 30, 420, an old man worn out by constant battling against "heresy" or the weaknesses of his own flesh. He was buried in the Church of the Nativity near his monastery, close to the graves of Paula and Eustochium. His remains were later moved to a church in Rome.

A discussion of his literary works is more appropriate to a book than a chapter. His output was enormous, consisting of hundreds of homilies, commentaries, translations, funeral eulogies, polemical writings, and letters, most of which were intended for public reading, and thus are really formal treatises expressing his views on many contemporary issues.

As a critical scholar and biblical exegete, Jerome was a Doctor of the Church par excellence, although one must realize that his talents lay strictly in interpretation, rather than in expounding doctrine. To doctrine he contributed almost nothing original.

One interesting work of his that had no precedent was *Famous Men*, a catalog of about 135 Christian authors, from the apostle Peter to himself. Composed about 393, the book's purpose was in part to disprove pagan charges that only ignorant people became Christians. Its defects include its plagiarism from Eusebius's *Ecclesiastical History* and the bias that governed the amount of space devoted to various men. While he dismissed Ambrose of Milan with a derogatory comment ("I shall refrain from giving my opinion on him, lest I should be accused either of toadying to or speaking the truth about him.") and John Chrysostom with one short sentence, he gives a long account of himself and a full list of his works. Be this as it may, the book is of immense value to the historian because it preserves the names of men and their writings that would otherwise have been erased from human memory.

Perhaps the outstanding contribution of Jerome to the church was his translation of the Bible into Latin, known today as the Vulgate. It addressed a problem that plagued the Western church: the multiplicity of different Latin versions, most of poor quality. Augustine wrote that it seemed as if everyone who knew a little Greek tried his hand at a Bible translation, and Jerome remarked that there were almost as many versions as there were manuscripts. He began with the Gospels, which he completed in 384. In 392 he completed a translation of the Psalms (called the Gallican Psalter) from the Septuagint, the Greek version of the Old Testament commonly used in the early church. As he began on other Old Testament books, however, he realized that it was imperative for him to master Hebrew and then translate from the original. Over the next fifteen years, amidst many distractions, he finished his great labor.

The Vulgate, a name his version received in the sixteenth century from the Latin phrase meaning "common (or) popular edition," was a great improvement in many respects for the Church. Certainly it had its defects, as in the translation of "repent" as "of penance," thus influencing people to believe that man must perform meritorious works in order to receive forgiveness. Actually, it was not all Jerome's work, for apparently the New Testament books other than the Gospels are simply a revision of a previous Latin version carried out by someone else. In addition, it was the Gallican Psalter that became common rather than his Hebrew Psalter. As for the apocryphal books, Jerome translated only two and felt they should not form a part of the Old Testament because the Jews rejected them. However, the Western church was attached to them, so they remained a part of the Latin Bible in the form of older versions.

The history of the Vulgate is a fascinating story in itself. Its text very soon developed variations, since copyists remembered the wording of the earlier version and, on purpose or not, made Jerome's work more like the translations it was supposed to correct. There were various attempts in the Middle Ages to standardize the Vulgate, notably by Alcuin in the time of Charlemagne and by the University of Paris in the thirteenth century. (The latter edition was the occasion when the Bible first received chapter divisions.) The Vulgate became the first book printed in Europe when the magnificent Gutenberg Bible came off the press in 1456.

In 1546 the Council of Trent declared the "ancient and vulgate version" to be the official Bible of the Roman Catholic Church, calling it "authoritative" among the Latin versions and declaring that "no one may make bold or presume to reject it on any pretext." Though some took this to mean that the Vulgate stood above the original Hebrew and Greek, most present-day Catholic scholars do not so interpret it, and translations from the original languages rather than from the Vulgate are now appearing. But to determine the original text of the Vulgate was another thing, and it was not until 1590 than an officially sanctioned Latin Bible was published, known as the Sixtine edition. It was full of errors, which was especially embarrassing since Sixtus V, who gave it full papal authorization, forbade the official use of any text that varied from his or included variants in the margins. Two years later, however, it was recalled and an extensive revision published under Clement VIII. In order not to slight Sixtus, the new edition was published with Sixtus's name on the title page (in spite of over 3000 changes) and a preface by Cardinal Bellarmine that falsely claimed that the first printing was full of misprints.

Since his death Jerome has been both fulsomely praised and bitterly denounced. Representing as he did some of the chief features of medieval Roman Catholicism—exaltation of monasticism and asceticism, superstitious devotion to Mary and the saints, legalism in morals and religious practice—Jerome was greatly admired throughout the Middle Ages. Unfortunately, his emphasis on the Scriptures and the diligent study of the original languages were not likewise valued as they should have been until the Renaissance and Reformation. While we may admire Jerome's talents and his learning, his flaming temper and unchristian actions lower our opinion of him considerably. Even Pope Sixtus V, looking at a picture of Jerome striking his breast with a stone, said, "You do well thus to use that stone: without it you would never have been numbered among the saints."

One scholar has well summarized Jerome's place in church history with these words: "Jerome lived and reigned for a thousand years. His writings contain the whole spirit of the church of the middle ages, its monasticism, its contrast of sacred things with profane, its credulity and superstition, its subjection to hierarchical authority, its dread of heresy, its passion for pilgrimages. To the society which was thus in a great measure formed by him, his Bible was the greatest boon which could have been given. But he founded no school and had no inspiring power; there was no courage or width of view in his spiritual legacy which could break through the fatal circle of bondage to received authority which was closing round mankind."

Was Jerome a saint in the sense of having found Christ as his Savior? One cannot know for sure. One can only grieve that a man who spent most of his life studying the Word of God could have missed the proper emphases of Scripture in so many areas of his life and practice. Certainly, Jerome was a man of great abilities, and great flaws.

In art Jerome is depicted (anachronistically) in a red cardinal's hat because of his service to "Pope" Damasus, or in a monastic cave with a lion at his feet, a pen in hand, and a book before him. The story about the lion from whose paw Jerome is supposed to have extracted a thorn is really the legend of St. Gerasimus, which has been transferred to Jerome.

Francis of Assisi

Of all the men and women whom the Roman Catholic Church can justly claim as her own, perhaps none is so universally attractive a personality as Francis of Assisi. His simple poverty, his humility, and his imitation of the life of Christ with disarming literalness give him an appeal across the centuries. Though unlearned and physically insignificant, he was a person of unusual charm and force of character, qualities that attracted even nonreligious people to him and won disciples from every segment of society.

In addition to, and perhaps as a result of, his personality and real life accomplishments, a body of legends grew up around Francis. The most famous collection, known as the *fioretti* or "Little Flowers," consists of numerous short accounts of unusual incidents supposed to have happened to Francis and his associates, each with a moral lesson faintly reminiscent of Aesop's *Fables*. They make delightful reading even for Protestants who will not experience even a slight temptation to accept them as proof of the validity of the Romanist doctrine that Francis espoused. They are on the same level as folk legends or heroic myths from any time or country.

Since the beginning of the twentieth century, when a French Protestant by the name of Paul Sabatier began publishing his detailed research on the real Francis, modern scholarship has gradually dispelled the myth and superstition surrounding the saint of Assisi. However, there will always be a gray area of uncertainty, and we shall never know beyond doubt what grains of truth lie buried in some of the miraculous stories so confidently and credulously reported by his close friends and other ostensible eyewitnesses.

Apart from his personal influence and his stature as a legendary hero, Francis figures large in the history of the Middle Ages because of the order he founded, the Franciscans. They were the first of the Mendicant ("Begging") Orders of friars, and along with the others—the Dominicans, Augustinians, and Carmelites—they are said to have saved the Catholic Church from collapse. Although the Roman Church entered the thirteenth century with the world-shaking activities of Pope Innocent III, before whom princes trembled, it was riddled by internal corruption in its hierarchy, challenged by numerous heretical sects, and threatened by a notable lack of spiritual energy and zeal among its constituents. The friars remedied the situation by initiating reforms, aggressively attacking heresy, and inspiring the people with new ideals. Europe in God's providence was not yet ripe for the thoroughgoing Reformation of the sixteenth century, which would expose and challenge the corruption of Romanism; so God allowed still another temporary measure to save it from falling under its own weight. Francis played a major role in this historical development.

Francis was born in Assisi, a small Italian town located about eighteen miles north of Rome, in 1181 or 1182. His mother, Pica, a well-bred woman, possibly of French descent, bore him in the absence of her husband, Pietro Bernardone, a wealthy cloth merchant who was out of the country on business. On Pietro's return, the boy was named Francesco, meaning "the Frenchman."

Francis grew up surrounded by plenty of money and the ease and entertainments that money made possible. His schooling was minimal, an inconvenience to be endured. At fourteen, Francis became an apprentice to his father in the cloth business, where he learned the language of trade and the art of making money.

Francis spent his leisure time as the leader of a band of carefree youths who called themselves "the Company of the Tripudiantes." Their purpose was to dance in public, acting out familiar ballads, some of them scenes from biblical history. Following the dancing, the revelers would invariably enjoy a lavish banquet at the expense of the one who was designated master of the club, usually Francis himself.

When Francis was twenty, war broke out between Assisi and a powerful rival city, Perugia. Francis joined the soldiers from Assisi in an assault on Perugia and was taken prisoner. He was held captive for a full year, during which time he astounded his fellow prisoners with his cheerful optimism. Nonetheless when Francis was released to return to Assisi, he was a different man. His experiences in war and the time spent in prison had made him more thoughtful.

His old friends welcomed him back enthusiastically, but no longer did the revels of the Tripudiantes delight him, nor did he take pleasure in the daily money-making schemes of his father's business. He was ill from privations suffered in prison and disillusioned by the life to which he had returned. Even when fully recovered, he could not escape the sense of depression that weighed on him. He became quiet and withdrawn. He was ripe for a change.

The conversion of Francis the reveler to Francis the saint involved a series of events. The first, on the authority of the Three Companions, later disciples of Francis, occurred during a banquet at which Francis was the disinterested host. Francis suddenly became very still, obviously transfixed by his own thoughts. His friends joked about his distraction, but later he reputedly experienced his first vision of "Lady Poverty," whom he described as "the most noble, rich, and beautiful fiancée you have ever seen."

Francis gradually withdrew from his former companions and began considering how he might best be employed. The call to knighthood appealed strongly to him: he decided to join the party of the French Count Gautier de Brienne in Apulia. With his love for fine clothes, Francis fitted himself out magnificently for his new quest.

Hardly had he set out when he met a nobleman reduced to rags following the wars, who looked with envy at Francis's splendid accoutrements. On impulse, Francis stripped himself of his armor and gave it all to the poor knight. Always generous, Francis had outdone himself. Without his equipment, he returned home to face the scornful amazement of family and friends. However, he was encouraged by dreams in which the Lord seemed to tell him to wait in Assisi for his true mission to be revealed to him.

At twenty-four, Francis was ready for another step in his "conversion," the rejection of self and its pride. He made a pilgrimage to Rome, the usual outlet for spiritual turmoil. In a shrine in Rome with other pilgrims, he watched the people throwing their offerings into the church coffers. Once again acting on generous impulse, Francis tossed his whole purse through the grating. Outside the shrine, Francis encountered a beggar whom he persuaded to exchange clothes with him in order that he might better understand the plight of the poor. He spent the day in a filthy, ragged tunic, begging for alms and associating with other beggars. He felt humiliated but also somewhat purged of his inner unrest.

On returning to Assisi, Francis spent his time among the town beggars and ministering outside the city to the lepers, the outcasts of his society. One day, Francis interrupted his works of charity to pray in the tiny, tumbledown chapel of San Damiano. As he prayed, he seemed to hear Christ say to him, "Francis, go and repair My house, which you see is falling down."

Francis, seeing clearly that the tiny chapel was in ruins, took the command literally. With incredible naïveté, he hurried home, gathered up a horse-load of expensive cloth, which he then sold, along with the horse, to raise the necessary funds to repair the chapel. Then he returned to San Damiano and offered the priest the money. The poor priest was hesitant to receive the great sum until Francis tossed the money on the window sill and left the chapel.

When Pietro Bernardone learned of his son's most recent folly, he was enraged and sought Francis to punish him. The young man was unrepentant of his deed, but did not resist when he father beat him and locked him up in his house. After a time, the elder Bernardone concluded that his son did not intend to renounce his religious fanaticism and restore to him the value of his cloth and horse. He therefore cited Francis for theft and disobedience before the city consuls, the only disciplinary option left to him.

Francis, calling himself a "servant of God," requested that he be tried before Bishop Guido. His trial took place on a cold afternoon in January of 1207 in the piazza before the Episcopal palace. Pietro Bernardone arrived with a group of friends and onlookers. The bishop ordered Francis to come forward to be accused. Following the citation of Pietro Bernardone's grievances, Bishop Guido addressed Francis:

"Even if you wish to serve the Church you have no right, under pretence of pious works, to keep the money that you have obtained in this way. Render then this money, evilly gotten, to your father."

Francis replied, "Willingly, Lord, and I will do even more."

He went inside the palace, removed his clothing and returned, almost naked, his clothes in a bundle in his hands. He spoke to the shocked assembly: "Until now I have called Pietro Bernardone my father, but now that I wish to serve God I return him not only his money, but also the clothes that I had from him. Now I can say no longer 'my father Pietro Bernardone,' but 'Our Father which art in heaven.'"

By his act, Francis formally renounced his rights as a son. He was legally disinherited. Francis left the trial alone, clothed in a laborer's smock that someone had given him. His father, "burning with rage and with an exceeding sorrow," as far as we know, never had any further contact with Francis, except to curse him from a distance when the two met by accident in Assisi's streets.

Francis, now penniless and free of all earthly ties, left the city limits and walked the highway, singing aloud, until he arrived at a monastery. There, known only as a wandering poor man, he worked as a kitchen boy in exchange for lodging and meager food.

Francis returned to San Damiano and for the next few years made frequent trips to Assisi to beg for stones to rebuild chapels needing repair. At first the people of Assisi ridiculed and abused "the crazy son of Pietro Bernadone," but eventually he won their affection by his cheerful manner, humble spirit, and eager work for the church. They began to boast of their local holy man. He became known as "Little Poor Man," *Il Poverello*. Francis lived during this time at San Damiano and subsisted on the fragments he could beg in Assisi.

In the spring of 1209, Francis reputedly received a commission for a different type of ministry. During a church service, Francis was struck by the text for the day from Matthew 10: "And as ye go, preach, saying, The Kingdom of heaven is at hand. . . . Provide neither gold, nor silver, nor brass in your purses, Nor scrip for your journey, neither two coats, neither shoes, nor yet staves: for the workman is worthy of his meat. . . . And when ye come into an house, salute it. And if the house be worthy, let your peace come upon it."

Francis, ever a literalist, found the words particularly relevant to his desires. Francis determined henceforth to carry no money. He threw away his shoes and walked barefoot. The Franciscan costume was conceived at this time. He adopted as his habitual dress an un-dyed woolen garment, tied with a rope at the waist. His greeting became "The Lord give you peace," and he began to preach, simply and without rhetorical device. It was because of his fervent preaching that others expressed a desire to join him in the espousal of Lady Poverty.

What was his message? Despite the multitudes of contemporary writings we have to choose from, there is not a single reference to specific content. We do know that he called men to repentance and to a life of simplicity and peace.

He exhorted his listeners to love God and their fellow men. He became renowned for his eloquence, for the passion of his delivery, for his uncanny ability to pierce into the heart. As his fame spread, he was invited to preach everywhere he went, even before the pope in

Rome. Tommaso da Celano provides for us a description of *Il Poverello* as a preacher:

> He was of middle height, rather short than tall. His skull was round, . . . his face a little elongated, . . . [his] eyes . . . black and limpid, the hair dark, the eyebrows straight, the nose regular, narrow, upright, the ears small, seeming to be always listening. . . . His manner of speech was soothing, burning, penetrating, his voice vibrant and sweet, clear and sonorous. His teeth were close-set, regular, white, his lips thin and narrow, his beard black and straggling, his neck thin. . . . He bore the very minimum of flesh.

Francis's magnetic personality soon attracted disciples. Because the group began to form without any official scheme of organization, there were no entrance requirements and no written guidelines. The public at first referred to them as "the Penitents of Assisi," until Francis originated the term *Fratres Minores*, or Lesser Brothers. The term *minores* had social significance because the citizens of Assisi were classed as *majores*, or rulers, and *minores*, peasants and workers without property. Francis wanted his men to be known as the servants of other men.

Soon it became necessary to establish a headquarters. In exchange for a quantity of fish and olive oil to be delivered yearly, the Benedictines of Mount Subasio "rented" the chapel of the Portiuncola to Francis. Surrounding the chapel, the Fratres Minores constructed crude huts in which to sleep.

The men slept and ate on the ground. During the day they devoted their time to prayer, manual work in the fields, and work in the leper colony. They relied on the fruit of their own labor as well as on charity for their food. "Alms are the heritage and right of the poor," according to Francis.

The Fratres Minores followed no set routine, but they were never idle. Francis insisted that "Brother Ass," as he called the body, must be kept busy, fed only the barest necessities, and deprived of the temptations of comfort.

Francis, overreacting to the barren and impractical scholasticism of his day, wrongly depreciated all pursuit of learning. "Brothers," he said, "You who are seduced by an excessive desire for knowledge, you will be found empty-handed on the day of tribulation. Cultivate virtue. For on that last day your books will be tossed out of the window."

According to one biographer, Francis advised against any reading: "He is happy who will make himself ignorant for the love of God." He refused to allow his brothers to possess books of their own, saying that once a brother possessed a psalter, he would soon be desiring a breviary; then he would haughtily tell another brother to bring it to him.

To Francis, the ultimate evil was the possession of money. He referred to money as "flies" and desired that his followers refuse even to handle coinage or accept money as alms. He explained to Bishop Guido the reason for his extreme position: "From property come disputes and lawsuits; it makes obstacles to the love of God and one's neighbor. So we won't possess any temporal goods in this world."

Despite the austerity of their circumstances, the Fratres Minores were admonished to be cheerful, even exuberant, as was Francis himself. Once he rebuked a downcast brother, "Why this sad face? Have you committed some sin? That concerns you and God alone. Before me and my brethren keep always a look of holy joy, for it is not decent, when in the presence of God, to show a gloomy, frowning air." He encouraged them to be *Joculatores Dei*, "God's Minstrels," and to express in song their inner joy.

Drawing on his background of secular singing and rhyme-making, Francis often composed impromptu songs, charades, and rhymes. Once when Francis and a brother, Leo, were on a preaching tour, Leo became ill and craved some grapes to eat. Francis, spying a vineyard, did not scruple to "borrow" several branches of ripe grapes. The owner of the vineyard caught him in the act and beat him with a stick. Francis took his punishment with his usual good humor and composed the following rhyme:

> *Brother Leo has very well eaten,*
> *But Brother Francis was very well beaten.*
> *Brother Leo is stuffed, tis true,*
> *But Brother Francis is black and blue.*

It was not long before Francis decided to request papal approval for his growing order. In this we see the seeds of the failure of his ideal, for the very evils he was seeking to remedy were woven into the fabric of the hierarchy. There were others in the Middle Ages, notably Peter Waldo and the Waldensians, who, like Francis favored a return to the simplicity of the Gospels, but unlike Francis, had the sense to realize that cooperation with and unqualified obedience to the pope and the hierarchy would mean the death of their reforms. Francis, it is true, taught that we must obey God, but he never saw the issue clearly enough to say with Peter Waldo, "We must obey God rather than men," and so to defy the pope. Instead Francis determined to gain an interview with the pope. Before going he composed his famous "Rule," consisting mainly of Scripture texts from the Gospels, which proposed that he and his followers continue to live without property as they had been doing. In 1210 a small group of Fratres Minores led by Francis set out for Rome. Their ragged leader was first questioned closely by the Cardinal of San Paolo in the Lateran Palace.

Legend has it that the pope, Innocent III, in the meantime had a vivid, symbolic dream of a poor monk who was propping up the crumbling Catholic Church by himself. The pope recognized the man of his dreams as Francis, who he thought "by his act and teaching [would] support the Church of Christ." Therefore, Pope Innocent III received Francis warmly, approving his Rule, and gave the plan his blessing, much to the horror of the cardinals. They felt the order needed to be more highly organized and its members under firm discipline in order to guard against rebellion and criticism against the established Church.

The Poor Men of Assisi returned to their home exulting in the apparent success of their mission and burning with enthusiasm to make converts. In the eyes of his medieval contemporaries, Francis was now "a true preacher, confirmed by apostolic authority."

The year 1212 also saw the emergence of a ladies' order under Francis's supervision. During Lent in 1211, a young girl of Assisi, Chiara di Favarone, known now as St. Clare, heard Francis preach and was greatly moved. She had always been deeply religious. Now, secretly and against the wishes of her aristocratic family, she began to meet with Francis. She implored him to accept her into the order, that she might renounce the world and possess only "Jesus Christ, the longed-for Spouse."

Francis was at this time twenty-eight, Clare seventeen. She was as beautiful as she was devout. She represented to Francis the feminine ideal of chastity and submission to Christ. The story of their meetings, with their potential for scandal, is almost apologetically set forth by the early biographers. Celano wrote about "that honeyed poison, familiarity with women, which leads even holy men astray." Nonetheless, the story of their spiritual kinship, which ended only with the death of Francis years later, presents no hint of indiscretion, except that the two defied religious convention.

In 1212 Clare and a companion left her home during the night by a little-used doorway and made their way to the chapel of Portiuncola, where the brothers were waiting to welcome them. Francis made arrangements for the two new "brides of Christ" to live at a Benedictine convent nearby. Eventually, the "Poor Clares," as she and the women who joined her were called, established their own order, were officially sanctioned, and made converts. Francis remained their spiritual father, preaching and directing their religious services. The ladies, on the other hand, sewed for him and supplied the feminine tenderness his life lacked.

Francis nurtured another friendship with a woman, this one a young widow, Lady Jacoba, who was drawn to Francis's teachings but was herself unable to renounce her property because she was responsible for the maintenance of several young children. Francis made Lady Jacoba an honorary member of the order, laying a precedent thereby for the Franciscan secular order, designed for those who wished to practice penance, charity, and comparative poverty, while maintaining conventional family ties. He affectionately nicknamed her "Brother Jacoba."

Groups of Franciscans were forming in many different locales. Organization remained loose, although the original Rule was revised, to Francis's dismay, to provide a somewhat more specific constitution. The brothers, widely scattered as they were, would travel to the Portiuncola once a year for a general meeting, or chapter. Francis would remind them on those occasions of their vows and encourage them to be good copies of their divine Exemplar.

In 1216 Francis again made a papal visit with an unusual request. Honorius III had succeeded Innocent III, and it was from him that Francis received the unprecedented Pardon for Assisi, or Portiuncola Indulgence. According to the story, as Francis was praying one day, a heavenly voice asked him what the Lord could do to relieve the burden from mankind. Francis, unashamed to offer God advice (unscriptural advice at that) suggested He might remove the weight of sin from penitent men. As a result of this dialogue, Francis was emboldened to ask the pope, "Christ's vicar on earth," for permission to extend to everyone who visited his church and confessed his sins to the priest a remission of the temporal punishment of the sins he had committed since his baptism. The pope granted it, Francis having insisted that the idea was divinely inspired. The cardinals feared that the new indulgence would hurt their commercial interests, but the pope kept his word and the indulgence went into effect. However, the cardinals were able to limit the indulgence to one day per year (August 2).

The Roman Catechism defines an indulgence as "a remission, granted by the Church, of the temporal punishment which often remains due to sin after its guilt has been forgiven." Temporal punishment, as opposed to eternal punishment, includes that which a person experiences in this life and in purgatory, which supposedly completes the purification of the soul so it can enter heaven. The practice assumes at least two important false doctrines of Romanism, namely, that the guilt and the penalty of the sins of believers were not fully paid for by Christ's death and that it is the business of the visible church on earth to punish or remit the sins of Christians. Francis's interest in gaining this indulgence for his chapel is one more indication of his whole-hearted agreement with the basic errors of Roman Catholic theology.

In 1219 Francis left Italy on a preaching tour of Egypt and Syria. At that time Crusaders were involved in a bitter struggle at Damietta, a powerful Egyptian city they had long held under siege. The Saracens had not surrendered, and the Crusaders were war-weary. The story goes that Francis came to confront the sultan of Egypt and thus win the war on a spiritual plane.

Francis and a brother crossed enemy lines outside the Crusaders' camp and were soon apprehended by Saracen soldiers. The two men continually cried out "Sultan, Sultan!" until their captors concluded that they were some kind of ambassadors from the Crusaders to the Egyptian leader.

Francis was ushered into the presence of the sultan, to whom he announced his mission of conversion. The sultan was moved by Francis's eloquent preaching and often invited him to speak before him, hoping to prolong his visit. Francis finally responded to an invitation that he remain at court: "If you and your people will accept the word of God, I will with joy stay with you. If you yet waver between Christ and Mohammed, cause a fire to be kindled, and I will go into it with your priests that you may see which is the true faith." The sultan's priests prudently declined the challenge, and Francis soon returned to the Crusaders' camp.

Francis returned to Italy to find his order departing from the ideals of his first Rule. He yearned for the days when he and his companions were free from administrative worries and could devote themselves to a simple life of work and prayer. From the standpoint of the papacy it was not in the interest of church authority to have a band of free-wheeling preachers roving about without some sort of control. According to one reconstruction of the events, Cardinal Ugolino, who later became Pope Gregory IX, was responsible for imposing strict discipline to ensure that the papacy could manage the order. Francis, though deeply disappointed, submitted to the wishes of the hierarchy, and his original Rule was set aside. Something of his spirit and ideals did survive among those known as the Observant or Spiritual Franciscans, but they were persecuted by the lax party known as the Conventuals. After several decades of fierce internal conflict over such issues as owning property and teaching in the universities, the order became in all important respects like other groups.

An important incident in Francis's life was the Christmas he spent at the town of Grecchio. Christmas was Francis's favorite day on the Church calendar, for he loved to think of the sacrifice the Incarnate Christ made to be born amidst poverty in Bethlehem. He announced to a friend that he would like to "make a memorial of that Child . . . and in some sort behold with bodily eyes the hardships of His infant state, lying on hay in a manger with the ox and ass standing by." Under his direction, a manger scene was recreated for everyone to enjoy during the midnight service at which Francis preached. The custom of reenacting the events of the Nativity owes much of its popularity to Francis's idea at Grecchio.

Part of the folklore for which Francis is most beloved concerns the saint and animals. Francis had a special fondness for, and rapport with, animals. Birds were not afraid to come to him, and legend tells us he even preached to them.

The most famous of the animal legends concerns Francis's taming of a wolf that had for some time terrorized the town of Gubbio, killing farm animals and even men. When Francis learned of the menace, he went alone to the wolf's lair and returned with the fierce animal trailing meekly behind him. He persuaded the citizens of Gubbio that the wolf was no longer intent on killing. Indeed, he had so "converted" the beast that it became the town pet.

Late in the summer of 1224, Francis took with him his closest friends and went to Monte La Verna, a rugged peak, where Francis is supposed to have experienced the climax of his years of meditation—the stigmata.[1] Francis began to contemplate the Lord's Passion. According to Bonaventura, he prayed: "Lord, I ask two graces of Thee before I die; to experience myself, as far as possible, the sufferings of Thy cruel Passion and to have for Thee the very love which caused Thee to sacrifice Thyself for us."

Suddenly, according to Bonaventura's legendary account, from "heaven a Seraph having six wings of flame swept down toward him. It appeared in the image of a man hanging on a cross [and was] Christ Himself . . . in this guise. It . . . fixed Francis with its gaze, then left, having imprinted on his flesh the sacred Stigmata of the Crucifixion."

From that time, Francis supposedly suffered from wounds in his hands, feet, and side, which he bandaged and kept hidden from view.

At forty-six, Francis was nearing the end of his life. His final achievement was the composition of his famous "Canticle of the Sun," which he completed while he lay near death at San Damiano under Clare's care. The Canticle, which has been translated often from its poetic Italian form, may be rendered fairly literally:

Most High, Omnipotent, Good Lord God.
Thine be the praise, the glory, the honor, and all blessing;
To Thee alone, Most High, they are due,
And no man is worthy to mention Thee.

Be Thou praised, my Lord, with all Thy creatures,
Especially our Brother Sun,
Who brings us the day and brings us the light.
And he is beautiful and shines with great splendor;
Thee, O Most High, he signifies to us.

Be Thou praised, my Lord, of Sister Moon and the stars;
In the heaven Thou hast formed them,
Clear and precious and lovely.

Be Thou praised, my Lord, of Brother Wind,
And of the air, and the cloud, and of calms and of all weather,
By which Thou givest life to all Thy creatures.

Be Thou praised, my Lord, of Sister Water,
Which is very useful and humble and precious and pure.
Be Thou praised, my Lord, of Brother Fire,
By which Thou hast lightened the night,
And he is beautiful and pleasant and very mighty and strong.

Be Thou praised, my Lord, of Our Mother the Earth,
Which sustains and keeps us,
And produces divers fruits with colored flowers and herbs.

Be Thou praised, my Lord, of those who pardon for Thy love,
And endure sickness and tribulation.
Blessed are they who peaceably shall endure,
For Thou, O Most High, shalt give them a crown.

The Canticle is more familiarly known in the translation by William Draper entitled "All Creatures of Our God and King." Francis, when he knew he would soon die, added the final stanza to his Canticle, in praise of "Sister Death."

Be Thou praised, my Lord, for our Sister Death,
From which no man escapes.
Woe to him who dies in mortal sin!
Blessed are they who are seen to walk in Thy holy will,
For the second death shall have no power to harm them.

Francis then dictated the Testament in which he summarized his life, conversion, and ministry, and added instructions for future generations of Franciscans.

Just before he died, he expressed a wish for some of the tasty almond cakes called frangipani that Lady Jacoba used to make for him. He desired that the brothers write to her to inform her of his state. However, before anyone could be sent with the letter, a brother announced her arrival. Although no woman was to enter the Portiuncola, Francis exclaimed, "Blessed be the Lord who has sent Brother Jacoba, for the Rule is not meant for her."

He could only taste the sweetmeats she brought, but she was a source of consolation to him during his dying moments. She also brought with her the necessary furnishing for his burial.

"He died singing," according to a biographer. "Be welcome, my

Sister Death," he called out, and added to his companions, "It is she who is going to introduce me to eternal life."

He died on Saturday, October 3, 1226, and was buried in view of a great crowd of mourners. Within two years he was officially proclaimed a saint. Shortly after his canonization, ironically enough, the Little Poor Man was re-interred in the sumptuous basilica that the Franciscan Brother Elias had built in his honor.

What do we conclude about Francis? If all one had to consider was his personal piety and devotion to the ideal of following Christ's example, he might be placed in a much different light. However, there is no evidence that he was some sort of medieval Protestant. While he had no sympathy with unjust or immoral prelates, he submitted nonetheless to the orders of the hierarchy and never doubted the authority of the pope. While he made literal obedience to the Gospels a major theme of his life, he never used the pure doctrine of the Word to attack the accretions of tradition and the subtle twisting of God's truth that dominated the Roman Church. He was liable to all the superstitions common in the thirteenth century. In short, he is a remarkable instance of a sincere and devout individual whose admirable characteristics shine through even though he was enmeshed in the errors of his day.

---

[1]The case of Francis was the first of the over three hundred recorded instances of the stigmata. Other famous Roman Catholics who reportedly received them include Catherine of Siena, Teresa of Avila, and Julian of Norwich. Even Roman Catholic writers do not consider them evidence of special holiness, and their similarity with certain pathological conditions demonstrates that there is nothing necessarily supernatural about the stigmata, even in cases where fraud is out of the question. Some hold that it is a sort of psycho-physical parallelism imposed on the body by the unconscious mind when the subject is in a state of ecstasy.

Joan of Arc

Joan of Arc—a name so familiar that no compilation of saints' histories is complete without her. Yet are we really that familiar with her life? Most of us have read a paragraph about her in our high school history book's account of the Hundred Years' War. Maybe you, like I, saw a filmstrip depicting her as a visionary, a glorious and inspired captain of the French who single-handedly engineered military victories, escorted the king to his coronation, and suffered martyrdom at the hands of the English.

During her brief career, Joan quickly became a living legend. Fanciful tales about her began to obscure the real Joan. The French saw her as a God-sent savior with miraculous powers; the English saw her as a witch and a heretic. By the time of her trial, the legends about her were so widely believed that her vigorous denials of them went unheeded.

To Catholics of the fifteenth century, visionaries and miracle-workers were more or less commonplace, although not so commonplace that they could not gain an audience with credulous captains and kings. But Joan was not the typical visionary. She was not a nun given to silent contemplation, nor was hers the language of mysticism. On the contrary, she was a robust teenager, a down-to-earth peasant with a sharp tongue, ready wit, and dogged determination. She was, above all, a person of energy and action. The matter of her visions is the one thing that sets her apart from other peasants of her day. These were not merely visions to be enjoyed and recounted as marvels. They were the stuff of which her career was made. She claimed that her every move was directed by her "voices." She followed the voices unquestioningly, and in the end, her allegiance to these voices condemned her to death at the stake.

What were they? Biographers speculate. Faithful Roman Catholics define them as the voice of God through special instruments. Skeptics explain them away as hallucinations but get bogged down where the "voices" correctly foretell future events. Joan's "voices" must remain inexplicable.

However, I can assert one thing with confidence: the "voices" were not messengers from God. With the closing of the canon of Scripture, God's special revelation to man was complete. The only "marching orders" the Christian requires are in the Word of God, with which Joan was not familiar. Her voices then, which for her represented God Himself, may have been as real as she described them, but they were not from God. The god she followed through life and agonizing death was a superstition of the Catholic Church.

One can deplore those superstitions without losing respect for the singular character of the young woman we call Joan of Arc. One cannot question her sincerity and her purity of mind and purpose. She is a sublime but simple example of dedication and courage.

Joan of Arc's life story played out at the climax of the Hundred Years' War. The name of the war is a misnomer, since the conflict lasted about 116 years (1337-1453) and there were many periods of relative peace during that time. The root of the conflict was that the English kings since William the Conqueror had held title to French lands such as Normandy and Aquitaine. The immediate cause of the war lay in Edward III's claim to the French throne after the death of his uncle, Charles IV of France, in 1328. For decades France was devastated not only by the war with the English, but also by outbreaks of civil war between nobles, the plague called the Black Death, bands of brigands aptly named *écorcheurs* ("skinners"), and peasant revolts in response to oppressive taxation.

The situation for France seemed particularly hopeless after 1392 when Charles VI began to experience long fits of insanity that sometimes made him violent. The country became engulfed in a bitter civil war between his cousin John the Fearless, duke of Burgundy, and Bernard, the duke of Armagnac. The latter was the close friend of the king's brother whom John the Fearless had assassinated. After the English won their famous victory at Agincourt in 1415 and John himself was killed in 1419, the Burgundians concluded a treaty with the English that recognized English claims to the throne. The Armagnacs, however, supported the third son of Charles VI, known as the Dauphin before his coronation and as Charles VII afterward. The English claimed that he was illegitimate, and he had his own doubts about the matter, since his mother had stayed away from her husband after the onset of his insanity. Thus the various parts of the country were under the control of three different powers: the English, who were strong in the north; the Burgundians, whose hereditary lands were in the west; and the Dauphin, supported by the Armagnacs in his tenuous hold on central and southern France.

The Dauphin's cause looked bleak indeed in 1427. When he was twenty-four, five years after his father's death, he was still uncrowned because the English and Burgundian armies held the cathedral city of Rheims, where the French had crowned their kings for hundreds of years. In addition, they held almost all the northern part of France. Joan's appearance at court came at a time when the situation was desperate enough to warrant unconventional measures.

Joan was born in 1412 in the small town of Domremy to ordinary peasants. Her father, Jacques, a plowman, enjoyed a good reputation among the people of Domremy and was one of several town leaders. Joan had three brothers and a sister. The children were not formally educated but learned from their mother, Isabelle, the Lord's Prayer, the Apostles' Creed, the Hail Mary, and much about the lives of favorite saints.

There was nothing out of the ordinary about Joan's early development. Like other little girls, she learned the crafts that would equip her to be a good housekeeper. At her trial in Rouen, she was later to boast that she feared no woman as her rival with the needle or spindle. Her childhood friends later remembered her to be exceptionally good and kind, hardworking, and a devoted Catholic.

By her later testimony, she was in her thirteenth year when she first heard the "voices" that were to direct her for the rest of her short life. She said that the voices first came to her at noon on a summer day while she was in her father's garden. From that time on, Joan heard daily from her "voices," whom she identified as the Archangel Michael, St. Margaret, and St. Catherine. Their messages became progressively more specific. They began by encouraging her to be a good girl, told her that God would aid her, and eventually instructed her to leave home and begin her mission: to raise the siege of Orléans and to see the Dauphin crowned. She never doubted the identity of her "angels," nor did she hesitate to follow their directives. Despite her initial anxiety when she learned what the voices expected of her, she told no one of her revelation for five years.

When Joan was sixteen, the voices became more urgent, directing her to present herself to the Dauphin. She made her first attempt to be introduced at court in May 1428. She left Domremy to visit her mother's cousin Durand Lassois and his wife in a small town two miles from Vaucouleurs, which was held by one of the Dauphin's garrisons. Her first obstacle was to convince "Uncle" Durand that he must help her achieve her goal of seeing the Dauphin.

Durand agreed to lead her to the commander, Robert de Baudricourt. When introduced, Joan did not waste time with preliminaries. "I have come," she announced, "by the order of Messire so that you shall tell the Dauphin to wait and not begin to fight his enemies." She said further: "The kingdom does not yet belong to the Dauphin, but Messire wishes that the Dauphin shall become king and that he shall rule the country under his guidance. Despite his enemies, the Dauphin shall become king, and it is I who will lead him to be crowned."

Baudricourt, understandably astounded, asked, "What Messire is it you are speaking of?"

"The King of Heaven," Joan replied simply.

Baudricourt, a hardened soldier not accustomed to taking orders from peasant visionaries, addressed Durand: "Take the wench back to her father and tell him to give her a good spanking."

That closed the interview, but did not end the matter. Joan returned home, but came back in January of 1429 when Durand's wife was due to give birth. Thus in January of 1429, seventeen-year-old Joan left home, never to return. As soon as she was able to be absent from the Lassois' home, she traveled to Vaucouleurs and was once again granted an interview with Baudricourt. He, along with others who had opportunity to observe her, was apparently convinced at least of her sincerity. This time he consented to send a report of her request to the Dauphin. During this interlude, Joan met a young soldier, Jean de Metz, to whom she said that she must appear before the Dauphin prior to mid-Lent "even if she should have to crawl on her knees." She gained his confidence and the promise of his help. He it was who claimed to have suggested to her that she dress as a man in order to travel inconspicuously and without tempting the soldiers with whom she would be fraternizing.

On February 12 Joan was authorized to set out for Chinon, the residence of the Dauphin. The leader of the expedition was Jean de Metz, and it included five others. Joan's mission had begun.

From this trip, we have a clear description of her appearance as a soldier. "As soon as these clothes and weapons were made, fitted and finished, Joan threw off . . . feminine attire: she had her hair cut round the head like a page, took shirt, trousers . . . and a short tunic down to about the knees, a tight-fitting cap, boots or leather gaiters, long stirrups, sword, dagger, hauberk, lance, and other weapons."

The absence of any reference in contemporary accounts to her beauty leads biographers to speculate that her face might have been rather plain. They reason that if she had been beautiful, someone certainly would have mentioned it. However, there are plenty of references to her fine figure. She was strong, remarkably so, to the extent that she could keep up with seasoned soldiers. She was graceful in the athletic sense, was a natural horsewoman, and could use weapons skillfully. Her black hair, cut short as it was, and her masculine attire seemed a strange contrast to her rather high-pitched and very feminine voice.

There was a quality in Joan's bearing that discouraged impropriety among her close associates. On this journey, as on succeeding ones, she slept fully clothed side by side with her men. Yet both Jean de Mertz and another soldier, Bertrand de Poulengy, testified that they felt no fleshly desires. Poulengy said, "I would never have dared to make her an improper proposal because of the virtue I felt she possessed."

Their journey took eleven days and required their passage through enemy-held territory. For that reason, they traveled at night. At a town several miles from Chinon, Joan addressed a letter to the Dauphin announcing their coming. News of "La Pucelle" ("the Maid," which was how she referred to herself) was already much discussed.

The king did not make haste to receive the self-styled savior of France. The delay in receiving her was typical of Charles VII. He was a weak and indecisive ruler, cowardly to the point of criminality, as events in the war and particularly those regarding Joan proved. As if to offset his character weaknesses, he cultivated his piety by attending Mass three times a day.

According to accepted legend, Charles disguised himself as one of his courtiers and milled about with the large assemblage that had gathered for the official reception of Joan at Chinon. It is accounted a miracle that the Maid was able to spot him immediately and present herself to him, thwarting his little deception and proving to him and to everybody that she possessed rare intuitive powers. Actually, it would not have required supernatural vision to select poor Charles from a roomful of people. She had undoubtedly heard him described. He was the embodiment of physical weakness. His nose was long and had a bulbous tip. His eyes were watery, and he had no eyebrows. His legs were bowed and spindly.

Yet Joan was not critical of either his moral or physical deficiencies. To her he was the Lord's anointed, for whom she was ready to risk her life. She addressed him: "Most illustrious Sir Dauphin, I have come and have been sent from God to bring help to the kingdom and yourself."

Legend tells us that at this juncture, Charles led her into a private chamber where she then was able to reassure him of her special calling by revealing to him the three subjects of a secret prayer he had been making to God. When the two were said to have rejoined the group in the audience chamber, it was noted that the Dauphin's face radiated his confidence in the Maid.

This is highly improbable in light of the fact that the Dauphin took pains to have Joan sent to Poitiers to be cross-examined over the course of several weeks before he expressed his satisfaction that she was divinely sent. It was to this thorough investigation at Poitiers that Joan appealed repeatedly during her later interrogation under the Inquisition at Rouen, but the records from Poitiers, which resulted in a favorable report of Joan, were never brought up as evidence.

However, history has preserved some of the details of the Poitiers investigation. Among her now-famous rejoinders to questions are the following examples:

When asked whether God could not just as well rid France of the English without battles, Joan responded, "In the name of God—the soldiers shall fight and God shall give them the victory." Another questioner wanted to know how she could expect the Dauphin to put an army at her disposal without her having first produced some sign to convince him. She retorted, "I have not come to Poitiers to produce signs. But take me to Orléans and you shall have signs."

When a churchman with a heavy local accent desired to know what language her "voices" spoke, she answered impudently, "A better one than yours."

Besides the investigation, there was at least one other incident at Poitiers that claims our attention. This is her letter to the English in which she warns them of her intentions. She begins by commanding them to withdraw immediately from all of the towns they are occupying in France. "If you do not do so," she continues, "you shall soon hear from la Pucelle, and it will cost you dear." She concludes her tirade, "If you refuse to believe this message from God and from the Maid, we shall strike wherever we find you and create such havoc that there has been nothing like it in France for a thousand years."

While at Chinon, Joan was often in the company of the Dauphin. He introduced her to a young prince, the Duke of Alençon, age twenty-three, who became one of her most loyal friends.

The Dauphin was eventually convinced that Joan was at least not a witch or an imposter. He decided to give her a chance to demonstrate the strength of her predictions to lift the siege of Orléans. After all, nothing could be lost by the attempt. He was shrewd enough to recognize the enormous popularity young Joan was achieving. If nothing else, she would be a tremendous boost to morale. He therefore consented to have her outfitted with her own armor and banner and sent her out with his troops. It is a mistake to believe that her position in any way resembled that of a commander-in-chief. History is clear that she was excluded, much to her annoyance, from all war councils, and from the actual forming of battle strategy, but it is equally clear that the military leaders followed her advice when she was able to convince them that it was of divine origin.

On April 28, 1429, Joan, with the Duke of Alençon at her side and an army of two or three thousand men, rode from Chinon toward Orléans. A larger army was to follow. Whether or not she was the official leader of the army, she was considered to be so by many. Jean D'Aulon, who followed her career faithfully as her horse master, said simply, "A woman has taken over the command in war." She was without doubt the religious head of the army—she saw to it that the men all confessed and ceased using bad language, and she dismissed the loose women who were accustomed to traveling with the soldiers.

When the army neared Orléans, Joan was informed that the plan was to enter the town with supplies for the people of Orléans and then to defer an attack against the English, commanded by Lord Talbot, until reinforcements arrived. Joan was furious at the delay, but agreed to remain quietly in Orléans until the entire army could be assembled.

On May 4, Joan was aware that the rest of the army had arrived, but was unaware of any immediate plan. She was resting when, apparently informed by the "voices" that she must now fight the English, she sprang up, demanded her horse and armor, charged through the east gate of the city, where she saw an English fort that the French were in the process of attacking. She threw herself into the thick of the fighting, and by her presence rallied the troops. The fort was taken with very little loss to the French.

On May 6 and 7, the French again attacked an English stronghold and their victory was decisive. The English were forced to capitulate and retreat. During the first day's fighting, Joan, who stayed in the fore of the attack, was wounded near the shoulder. She wept from the pain, but insisted on pulling the arrow out herself and prescribed her own treatment. Against advice, she rushed back into the battle, shouting encouragement to the men.

The wound was no surprise. She had predicted it to the Dauphin while still at Chinon, and the prophecy was common knowledge a full month before the battle at Orléans.

Joan's next important goal was to see the Dauphin crowned king at Rheims. But before this could be accomplished, it was necessary to clear out English resistance in the Loire River district. The French forces took the towns of Jargeau, Beaugency, and Patay. The time was ripe for an offensive against the English at Paris, but rather than press their advantage, the French armies retired to Sully-sur-Loire where the Dauphin awaited them. The coronation of Charles VII took place on July 17, 1429. Joan, holding her proud banner, stood near the altar. Her second major objective had been achieved.

After his coronation, Charles seemed to abandon any idea of attacking Paris. Joan, while always outwardly loyal to her sovereign, entreated him to make a decisive move while the time was propitious for a French victory. He, however, was extremely reluctant to undertake a new campaign, probably because he was involved in negotiations with the Burgundians in Paris that he hoped would result in a peaceful settlement. Joan's response to talk of peace was always, "There can never be peace with Burgundy except at the point of the lance." Nevertheless, an uneasy peace was achieved by a series of short-term treaties between Charles and Philip, Duke of Burgundy.

Joan was forced to be idle, and she could not have been unhappier. During the autumn months she engaged in a few half-hearted skirmishes for minor strongholds, but neither side accomplished much by their efforts.

On August 25, Charles allowed Joan to leave for Paris along with the Duke of Alençon and one detachment. Charles envisioned it only as a sort of reconnaissance mission. He promised to follow shortly after with more troops to launch the offensive.

The days passed into September and still the king hesitated. Meanwhile, Joan was constantly looking for a chance to attack. On September 5 the king finally started out for Paris, but by this time, the English were well warned and armed against the inevitable attack by Charles and the girl-soldier whom the English firmly believed was a sorceress.

The battle began on September 8. Joan took an active part in the assault and was wounded in the calf. She sat on the ground and called to her men not to give up. She herself refused to concede failure despite the losses the French were suffering when confronted by the obvious English superiority. The next day, Joan and Alençon threw a bridge across the Seine and were optimistic about their chances of scoring a victory, when orders came from the king that they were to withdraw immediately and retire to the nearby town of Saint-Denis. The king's men, to make sure the attack would not be renewed, destroyed the bridge the army had planned to use during the attack.

Joan must have been profoundly demoralized by this debacle at Paris and by the king's duplicity. She deposited her sword at a church in Saint-Denis. The army disbanded, and all of her faithful friends returned to their homes and families. Joan was completely alone. She was virtually a prisoner in the king's court, and, what was worse, she was now without a sense of purpose or mission.

Joan spent some winter months at Bourges in the company of her hostess, Marguerite La Touroulde. The king paid Joan a regular salary. She was now in possession of considerable wealth, which enabled her not only to live comfortably, but also to give gifts and alms. Charles further honored her by conferring nobility upon her and her family. The family took the official name "*du Lys*" (of the Lily).

Joan cared little for such honors. Her voices had told her that she was to have only a year and a little more to accomplish her mission. Her frustration increased with her enforced idleness.

In the spring, the Duke of Burgundy moved to take the strategic town of Compiègne. Charles was spared having to involve himself because Joan determined to go to its assistance. She was accompanied only by a small troop of men and her squire, Jean d'Aulon. She was in Compiègne in May 1430. Her voices had told her that this was to be her last confrontation.

On May 23 Joan led an attack and twice beat back the Burgundians. The English had arrived to reinforce their allies, however, and they surrounded the small group of French. Joan's men panicked and fled. Joan, remaining behind, determined to fight. She was overtaken by an enemy soldier, dragged from her horse, and forced to surrender. From that moment on, she was a prisoner.

No one, from the local garrison to Charles VII, made a move to save her. The king did not even venture to pay the price of her ransom. She, who had sacrificed herself repeatedly in his behalf, was left to her fate.

Her captors, for their part, were as happy as if they had captured a king. She was imprisoned under constant guard and was treated kindly at first, almost as a celebrity, but after two attempts to escape, she was removed to more secure quarters at Arras, a Burgundian town. The University of Paris, which sided with England and was the bastion of Catholic theology, claimed that Joan was a heretic and must be tried under the Church's jurisdiction. She was, therefore, removed to Rouen, the largest city after Paris and an English possession, for her trial. She arrived on December 23, 1430.

In order to give the trial the appearance of fairness, the English renounced their rights of trying her to Frenchmen who would serve their cause. Furthermore, the trial was to be an ecclesiastical one, calculated to convict her on charges of heresy that would gain the assent of every good Catholic.

Before a formidable group of church doctors, Joan responded to questions that would have baffled theologians. By prior arrangement, the judge, Pierre Cauchon, set verbal traps in order to secure damning testimony from her own lips. During the months she was incarcerated, she was denied the privileges of attending church services. The court's one concession was to assign her a confessor, who presented himself as a friend and so gained her confidence, but who was actually a spy who betrayed her to the judges.

Day after day she faced her accusers with their endless and seemingly irrelevant questions. Her keen wit never failed her, although she would sometimes evade or refuse to answer questions she perceived to be tricks.

Many of her spirited answers have become justly famous. Her intelligence surprises readers accustomed to thinking of medieval peasants as backward and inarticulate. For instance, when asked whether she considered herself to be in a state of grace, she avoided the trap of either presumption or admitting guilt by replying, "If I am not, I pray to God to make me so, and if I am, may God keep me so."

She was asked whether the saints of her visions hated the English, to which she replied, "They love whatever God loves, and hate whatever He hates." They asked her whether they spoke French or English. Her patriotic response was, "How could they speak English when they are not on the side of the English?" They asked her if Michael was naked or clothed when he appeared to her. She retorted with wonderful impudence, "Do you imagine God could not afford to dress him?"

She was interrogated about her choice of men's clothing, which, they reminded her, the Bible forbids, and concerning the harmless pastimes she enjoyed with friends during childhood. Some of these were games about "fairies" that had been handed down for centuries. The judges, at a loss to uncover anything incriminating from her youth, desired to prove that she had a history of witchcraft. She scorned those suggestions as sheer nonsense. She also denied the suggestions that she had allowed people to venerate her or that she had accomplished miracles, reports of which were already numerous.

In March of 1431 she was made to answer to the seventy formal articles brought against her, known as the Act of Accusation. These included the same weary allegations to which she had already responded, such as her dabbling with magic, her refusal to dress as a woman, her consorting with evil spirits, her shedding of blood in war. The articles were eventually condensed to twelve. Joan remained firm in her denial of any offense against the church. "I am a good Christian. I will answer all these accusations before God."

On May 24 her sentence was read to her, and she was urged to recant or be burned. Joan, who had always feared fire, was overcome by a terror she had never known before. She repudiated her "errors" and recanted. Her life was spared, but she was taken back to the same tower where she faced lifelong imprisonment.

On May 27 she withdrew her recantation, saying, "Ever since Thursday my voices have said to me that I did something very despicable when I confessed that I should not have done what I have done. What I said or retracted was only because of my fear of the stake."

"A relapsed heretic," she was again sentenced to death at the stake. When she was informed of her sentence, she burst into tears: "Oh, that I should be treated so cruelly. . . . I would sooner have my head cut off seven times than be burnt in this manner. . . . Before God the highest judge, I appeal."

When Cauchon entered, she cried out, "My Lord Bishop, it is you who murder me."

She was conveyed in a cart to the town square where a huge crowd had gathered. A theologian of the University of Paris read her a final admonition. Before the stand where the stake was erected was a board bearing these words: "Joan, who calls herself the Maid, liar, evil-doer, seducer of the people, sorceress, witch, blasphemer of God, denier of the faith of Jesus Christ, idolater, fallen, evoker of evil spirits, apostate, schismatic, heretic."

Joan began to pray, invoking the aid of Jesus, her saints, and the Virgin Mary. To the crowd she called tearfully, "I beg you to pray for me," and to the assembled priests, "I beg you to say a Mass for me."

Many wept. Others, irritated by the delay, clamored for her death. When she was fastened to the stake, she requested that someone hold a crucifix before her when the fire was lighted. The flames enveloped her. She did not scream or groan, but was heard to cry out, "Jesus!"

After her death, a secretary to the English king was said to have mourned: "We are lost. It is a saint we have burnt."

Joan, burned as a heretic by the Inquisition, was nonetheless a loyal Catholic who never questioned the authority of the Church and had outspokenly condemned the "heresies" of Jon Hus and Jerome of Prague, two noble Bohemian martyrs who were burned some fifteen years before for resisting the errors of Romanism. Her death was more a political execution than a judgment of heresy. Joan's trial was intended not only to discredit her, but also the king in whose service she served. For that reason, it was politically expedient to clear her name. Charles VII therefore ordered a retrial, called a rehabilitation, which cleared Joan of all wrongdoing twenty-six years after her death. Pope Calixtus III revoked the former sentence, which was declared illegal on several points of procedure.

Joan was formally canonized on May 6, 1920, by the same Church that burned her, but had been for centuries revered as the patron saint of France. Today we may admire Joan for her courage, her patriotism, and the firmness of her convictions; we may pity her fate at the hands of dishonest and unjust judges; we may be intrigued by her character and deeds that portray her as an enigma of history; but she was, after all, caught in the superstitions of medieval Romanism and deluded by that unscriptural system.

Teresa of Avila

Teresa Sanchez Cepeda D'Avila y Ahumada was born at dawn on March 28, 1515. Two years later, Martin Luther posted his ninety-five theses against the sale of indulgences on a cathedral door in Germany. Teresa, having grown up in a stronghold of Catholicism—medieval Spain—and absorbed much of its fanaticism, was horrified by the Lutheran "heresy." She dedicated all of the energies of her adult life to bring about the counter-reformation in her beloved Catholic church.

The story of Teresa of Avila is one of intense devotion to a cause, a cause she believed to be the work of Christ through her. The tragedy is that her cause was not the cause of the Christ of the Bible. Her Christ was the subject of her famous mysticism—visions, voices, and special revelations. Her Christ emerged from centuries of Catholic speculation and formal tradition. Her Christ was not the Omnipotent Redeemer of Scripture. He was only a part of a huge system of penance, ritual, and good works fabricated to save a soul from perdition. Teresa relegated the Bible to its "proper" sphere—the friars and the clergy. When a Bible-carrying novice sought admission to one of Teresa's convents, Teresa exclaimed indignantly, "Away with you, wench, and your Bible!"

Avila, the place of Teresa's birth, is an ancient, fortified city of old Castile. Nearly four thousand feet above sea level, Avila boasts one hundred towers, which compete with the surrounding mountains. Its climate is harsh, as is the terrain around it. This is not the sunny, carefree Spain of romantic literature. Castile is a province of granite, and its people are rugged and serious.

The Cepeda family was one of the noblest in Avila. Teresa's father, Don Alonso, brought up his family within the walls of an imposing palace. His first wife bore him three children before her death. His second wife, Beatriz de Ahumada, Teresa's mother, reared his first three children along with nine of her own. She was married at fourteen, and she died at thirty-three. Teresa remembered her as a beautiful woman whose one recreational outlet was reading romances of knight errantry and noble martyrdom. Don Alonso, a pious man, disapproved of frivolity and would have objected strongly to his wife's pastime had he been made aware of it.

Teresa shared her mother's love for romances. "So completely was I mastered by this passion," she wrote, "that I thought I could never be happy without a new book." Don Alonso had taught the child to read in order to share with her his library, which included serious classics by such authors as Cicero and Seneca, as well as devotional literature by churchmen.

Teresa, age seven, and her favorite older brother, Rodrigo, eleven, were most impressed by the tales of adventure they read in their mother's room. They resolved to run away to Africa, where they sincerely hoped they would be gloriously martyred. They made their escape from the palace and through a city gate, but met with a kinsman who spoiled their plan by returning them to their family. Rodrigo was quick to lay all of the blame for the escapade on "the little one," who he said wanted to die as quickly as possible in order to see God sooner.

Teresa's apparent zeal for God waned as she grew older. Her interests shifted from heaven to the pleasures of youth and fun-loving company. Her warmth and vivacity attracted others to her. She loved to converse: "I always had the defect of making myself understood only with a torrent of words." Usually sweet-natured, she confessed to a bad temper: "The Devil sends so offensive a spirit of bad temper that I think I could eat people up." She was ardent: "When I desire anything I am accustomed naturally to desire it with some vehemence."

She was also beautiful. Rather tall and somewhat plump, she had thick, curly dark hair, white skin, and good color. Her teeth were white and even, and her eyes round, black, and full of laughter. Her hands and feet were small and exceptionally pretty. Teresa recorded that she used her good looks to their best advantage during her teen years: "I began to make much of dress, to wish to please others by my appearance. I took pains with my hands and hair, used perfumes and all vanities within my reach, and they were many, for I was very much given to them." She obviously retained a bit of her youthful vanity in old age because once when an inept painter did a portrait of her, she teased him: "May God forgive you, Fray Juan! What I have had to suffer at your hands, and after all to paint me ugly and blear-eyed!"

Nor did she ever lose her attention to cleanliness, an unusual trait among "saints" before the modern period. Her clothes, and later her ragged habits, were always meticulously clean. A contemporary wrote that "her coifs and tunics never smelt of sweat or any other unpleasant smell, like those of other people."

Teresa recalled her youth as being characterized by great wickedness, although we have no record of grave immoralities. "I was very adroit in doing anything that was wrong." Her father, now solely responsible for her upbringing since the death of Beatriz when Teresa was thirteen, decided to remove her from the ungodly influence of her companions by placing her in an Augustinian convent school.

At sixteen, then, she entered a convent, without any idea that she would become a nun when her brief stay there was over. While she was not unhappy there, she was violently opposed to the idea of taking vows. Yet, she said, she was also "afraid of marriage," and in the sixteenth century, the convent was her only honorable option.

She returned home after eighteen months, but fear of damnation haunted her until she concluded she must become a nun or forfeit her soul. She stressed in her autobiography that she was far more motivated by "servile fear" than by love at this point in her life.

Against her father's wishes, she committed herself to the Carmelite convent of the Incarnation. Her first years there were interrupted by serious illness—fainting fits and heart seizures. Also, at his period, and significantly so from a psychological point of view, she began to have visions and hear voices. For the next two decades she progressed in mysticism until her fame was widespread. She did not at first welcome her special visitations—in fact, she considered them embarrassing and inconvenient, particularly when they came upon her (in seizure form) in public. For some time, she was troubled lest her visions be of the devil. It was because of these doubts that she began to record her recollections of the visions in order to submit them to the scrutiny of her confessors, who eventually convinced her not to fear their origin.

Historians count Teresa as one of the prominent leaders of mysticism. Though difficult to define, mysticism is the belief that the individual can experience direct contact or even union with God, usually by assuming a totally passive mental attitude, practicing deep meditation, and progressing through various stages of spiritual experience. It dispenses with all intermediaries and proposes that one's knowledge of God can go beyond merely seeing His work in daily life or learning about Him in the Bible. The mystics, whether Christian or pagan, seek immediate spiritual experiences that transcend the normal operations of mind and body, and they often claim fantastic visions, miraculous exhibitions of divine power, and extra-biblical revelations. Mysticism has a basis in the necessity of every man to have a personal relationship with God, but it bypasses the objective truths of Scripture and glorifies subjective experiences. It lays its practitioners open to deception by Satan or by self, and it sometimes promotes an unhealthy introspection and a self-centered attitude.

These defects in mystical thought and practice find ample demonstration in Teresa's life. Her mysticism, far from showing to her the truth of the universal priesthood of the believer, as taught by her Protestant contemporaries, bound her more closely to the superstitious errors of Romanism. It is foolish to suppose that she found true fellowship with God. Plausible explanations of her supposedly miraculous experiences are easily found in medical annals, which reveal the connection between conditions of the body and mind and these types of mystical raptures. Suffice it to say that Teresa's visions seemed to be associated almost always with ill health, and she describes the subjects of her visions—demons, legendary saints, of Christ Himself—in terms consistent with the literature and art of the period with which she was familiar. They were not new revelations from God. Most likely, they were the product of her subconscious mind and her passion, accentuated on many occasions by physical mortifications.

Her autobiography reveals much about her personality and theology. She did have an extremely practical turn of mind, unlike many mystics, but her mysticism definitely stayed within the bounds of Roman Catholic teachings. She lists the results of mystical prayer as devotion to "the Queen of Heaven," who propitiates God; invocation of the saints; and greater reliance on the power of the sacraments. She claimed that the mental and bodily pain she underwent in her mystical experiences purified her soul from "the dross . . . which would have to be burnt away in purgatory" and that her prayers had delivered so many souls from purgatory "that were I to speak of them I should only weary myself and my reader." She frequently experienced trances and visions while attending mass. For instance, once after the wafer was placed into her mouth, "I verily believed that my mouth was all filled with blood; and my face and my whole body seemed to be covered with it, as if our Lord had been shedding it at that moment." This 'benefit" was bestowed on her, she thought, "because I have been in the habit of going to communion, if possible, on this day [Palm Sunday] for more than thirty years, and of laboring to prepare my soul to be the host of our Lord." Such Romanist nonsense is evident everywhere in her writings.

She pitied the Lutherans, who, she said, had fallen from the salvation they once had through baptism and were deluded by Satan because they rejected the use of images. She emphasized the veneration of Mary and the saints. After her mother died she prayed that the Virgin would be a mother to her and later felt that prayer to be a source of great benefit. Among the saints her special patron was Joseph. She wrote of him, "I cannot call to mind that I have ever asked him at any time for anything which he has not granted," and added the blasphemous explanation, "Our Lord would have us understand that, as He was Himself subject to him upon earth—for St. Joseph, having the title of father, and being His guardian could command Him—so now in heaven He performs all his petitions." This type of pagan reasoning is the true basis of prayers to the saints.

Teresa placed great store in going to confession, but in spite of her profuse expressions of self-abnegation and unworthiness she lacked a true sense of the depths of human depravity. The Roman Catholic distinction between venial sins, which will be removed in purgatory, and mortal sins, which result in damnation if unconfessed, was very important to her. She continually fusses over "venial" sins as "my many vanities" but fails to understand that every sin, however insignificant, is as much worthy of eternal punishment as a so-called mortal sin, since they both arise from a corrupt nature. In light of her constant concern over peccadilloes, her statements, such as, "I am the most wicked and the basest of all who are born of women," smack of false humility. The impression is made stronger by noticing her detailed accounts of special divine favors and graces she received through supernatural visions. She seems to set herself up as the one with an inside line to the Almighty, the one who can communicate His will to the rest of us benighted souls.

For over twenty years, Teresa led the semi-retired life of the convent of the Incarnation. There, the discipline being quite relaxed, she could entertain guests in the convent parlor, decorate her cell as she desired, and even adorn herself with jewelry if she chose. She began to be dissatisfied with her spiritual progress. About 1555 Teresa became acquainted with the original Rule of the Carmelites, who foolishly traced their history back to the time of Elisha when, they say, a group of anchorites established themselves with him in the caves of Mount Carmel.

Carmelites, who led a life of contemplation and poverty, were a recognized community by the twelfth century. Their vows of abstinence and solitude were deemed too strict, and by order of Eugenius IV (1431-1447) the rule had been relaxed. Carmelite communities for men and for women multiplied across Europe and were full of abuses and laxity by the time Teresa entered the Incarnation.

Teresa became impressed that her mission was to leave the Incarnation and to found convents that would adhere to a stricter rule, consistent with the demands of earlier Carmelites. Her ideal was absolute poverty and withdrawal for purposes of contemplation, penance, and particularly, for prayer, which she felt to be much needed in light of the threat to the Roman Church by Protestantism. Furthermore, she directed that new foundations be supported through public alms.

She knew instinctively that her work could best be accomplished by new foundations. She chose not to attempt reform in complacent, wealthy convents whose inclinations were vastly different from hers.

When she left the Incarnation in 1562 and founded the first convent of the Reform, St. Joseph's, she provoked a storm of hostility and protest among religious leaders who sensed in her effort to reform the Carmelites an attack upon the corruption of the whole Church system. For the next twenty years she traveled extensively, setting up convents and winning converts to her cause, even among her strongest opponents. More remarkable, perhaps, than her energetic work of reform was her skill in diplomacy, her tact, strength of purpose, and legendary charm. Without these qualities, the most tireless effort would have been unsuccessful.

The Carmelites of the Reform came to be known as Discalced, or "barefoot," whereas the observers of the Mitigated Rule were Calced, or "shod." At one point, opposition to the Reform became so violent that Teresa was nearly defeated. She was accused of being a gadabout and "a disobedient contumacious woman who promulgates pernicious doctrine under the pretense of devotion; leaves her cloister against the order of her superiors and the decrees of the Council of Trent; is ambitious and teaches theology as though she were a doctor of the church, in contempt of the teaching of St. Paul who commanded women not to teach." However, during the crisis, the pope forever settled the dispute by granting the Discalced Carmelites independent status.

This status was conferred in 1580. By this time, Teresa, an old woman, had delegated much of her authority over the foundations to others. While she was responsible for the women's reform, she relied on several men to effect change in the monasteries. Among these were Juan de Yepes, later known as John of the Cross, and Gracián, a young man for whom she bore a great affection. John of the Cross was small of stature, and one of Teresa's favorite jokes was to refer to the two men as her "friar and a half."

When she was too ill to oversee the details of her convents, she continued her administration through her correspondence, which was vast. From her letters, of which hundreds are extant, we see her nature best exposed. They are full, not of weighty, spiritual matters, but affectionate advice for those she loved, such as how to dress in cold weather, or amusing anecdotes from her journeys. Her style is delightfully chatty (though somewhat diffuse), down- to-earth, direct, and full of homey references.

The accounts of her contemporaries regarding her prayer life are interesting, more notable to our minds for her wit rather than for her reverence or humility. Once when she felt herself charged by God with a message to deliver to a particular person, she retorted, "Why dost Thou give me this trouble? Canst Thou not speak directly to that person?" On another occasion, when she had just endured a hazardous river crossing, she was heard to mutter, "It seems impossible that, after having . . . dedicated all my labors to thee, thou shouldest treat me thus." Whereupon she heard a voice, "Thus do I treat my friends!" To which she responded, "For this reason hast thou so few."

By the end of her life, when her convents were flourishing and her controversial reform was exonerated by the church, she was hailed by many Roman Catholics as a saint. To this veneration she responded: "I have been told I am good looking and I have not demurred. I have been told I'm brilliant and I have not contradicted, but a saint—oh no." Protestants would agree, though for a different reason.

In the fall of 1582, Teresa, now old and feeble, was requested to visit the young daughter-in-law of the Duchess of Alba, who was expecting a baby shortly. Teresa and her companions hurried to reach the young woman's side, but word came as they were en route that the lady had been safely delivered. "Thank God," said Teresa humorously, "this saint will no longer be needed."

Teresa lodged in Alba in one of her convents, where she was welcomed warmly by "her daughters." There she succumbed to the illness that took her life. In her weakness, she pled for pardon for her sins, repeating often, "After all, Lord, I am a daughter of the Church." Barely coherent for her last few hours, she murmured the words of the Psalmist: "Cor contritum et humiliatum Deus, non despices" ("A broken and a humble heart, God, you will not despise").

A dear friend, Fray Antonio, interrupted her thoughts by asking her whether she wished her body to be taken to Avila for burial. "Must you ask that, my brother? She replied. "Will they not give me a little earth here?"

She died the evening of October 4, 1582, at the age of sixty-seven. She left behind her a country of admirers. She was formally canonized in 1622 by Pope Gregory XV and her feast day established as October 15. In 1970 she was made a doctor of the Church by Pope Paul VI. Her books are recognized as masterpieces of Spanish literature and of mystic theology. She wrote an autobiography entitled *The Life of Mother Teresa of Jesus*, and her *Book of the Foundations* describes her labors for the Reform. Her works describing spiritual progress toward God are *The Way of Perfection*, *The Interior Castle*, *Spiritual Relations*, *Exclamations of the Soul to God*, and *Conceptions of the Love of God*. Thirty-one poems and 458 letters are also preserved.

Romanism teaches that a saint's holiness gives to him or her the power to perform miracles. Romanism teaches further that this power is communicated to items the saint uses frequently and that it remains in the corpse after death. Consequently, relic seekers often tear the saints' bodies to pieces, and so it happened to Teresa. The nuns exhumed her after nine months, and Father Gracián cut off her left hand. Later, Gracián and some other friars stole her body (except for the remains of her left arm) and took it to Avila. They afterwards returned it, but when the nuns exhibited it publicly, the eager crowds mutilated it further. Finally in 1750, after five exposures and reburials, Teresa's fragmented body was securely entombed above the High Altar in the rebuilt and richly ornamented church at Alba, where it is finally safe from the excesses of Roman Catholic superstition.

What should we think of Teresa of Avila? The philosopher and psychologist William James, though no friend of orthodox Christianity, gives an interesting evaluation of Teresa in his *Varieties of Religious Experience*. He admires her talent: she "possessed a will equal to any emergency, great talent for politics and business, a buoyant disposition, and first-rate literary style. She was tenaciously aspiring, and put her whole life at the service of her religious ideals," yet he felt "pity that so much vitality of soul should have found such poor employment." For all her supposed depth of feeling, she was superficial, self-interested, and full of false humility. Although she claimed "unheard-of personal favors and spiritual graces from her Saviour," of what benefit were they to others?

> In the main her idea of religion seems to have been that of an endless amatory flirtation—if one may say so without irreverence—between the devotee and the deity; and apart from helping younger nuns to go in this direction by the inspiration of her example and instruction, there is absolutely no human use in her, or sign of any general human interest.

He then makes a penetrating comparison with her contemporary Martin Luther:

> We have to pass a similar judgment on the whole notion of saintship based on merits. Any God who, on the one hand, can care to keep a pedantically minute account of individual shortcomings, and on the other, hand can feel such partialities, and load particular creatures with such insipid marks of favor, is too small-minded a God for our credence. When Luther, in his immense manly way, swept off by a stroke of his hand the very notion of a debit and credit account kept with individuals by the Almighty, he stretched the soul's imagination and saved theology from puerility. So much for mere devotion, divorced from the intellectual conceptions which might guide it towards bearing useful human fruit.

This final group of saints represents the many legendary or quasi-legendary names included on the list of saints. Most of them are well known through charming legends, traditional customs, works of art, and fine music. Some of them may indeed have lived, and we may possess a few reliable facts about them, but the lavish embellishment of tradition has relegated them to the shadowy land of legend.

Perhaps these tales prompted Ambrose Bierce to define a saint as "a dead sinner revised and edited."

These charming tales enrich our culture and delight the casual reader as do all folk legends. They interest and amuse us, but the fabulous nature of the stories disqualifies them as a means to edify the reader. Some of the subjects of the legends may have had hope in Christ for eternity and may have died heroically for Him, but we must regard the legends connected with their names as separate and unknown entities from their true life histories.

Part Three

Cecilia
Christopher
Valentine
Lucy
Nicholas of Myra
Wenceslas

Cecilia

The day was comen of her marriage,
She ful devout and humble in her corage,
Under her robe of gold, that sat ful faire,
Had next her flesh yeclad her in an haire.
And while that the organs maden melodie,
To God alone thus in her heart sang she;
O Lord, my soule and eke my body gie
Unspotted, lest that I confounded be.
–Geoffrey Chaucer, "The Second Nonnes Tale"

It was Cecilia's wedding day, as the legend goes. The setting was imperial Rome in the second century A.D. The reigning emperor was Marcus Aurelius, who is famous today for writing his *Meditations*, a classic work of Stoic philosophy. Though a very moral man in contrast to most of the late Roman emperors, he despised and persecuted the Christian church. The heroine of our story was a young woman of noble birth whose parents had embraced Christianity. Cecilia herself was devout, having fasted regularly and worn the coarse garment of penance under her patrician robes. Secretly, Cecilia had made a vow of chastity to God. Ignorant of her vow, Cecilia's father had arranged a marriage between her and Valerian, also a patrician, but a pagan.

Cecilia, calm despite her predicament, sat apart while the wedding guests enjoyed the festivities. She prayed for help and sang to God in her heart. Later, when the newlyweds were alone, Cecilia surprised her young bridegroom with the news of her secret vow of chastity. She told him, as Chaucer relates it,

I have an angel which that loveth me,
That with gret love, wher so I wake or slepe,
Is redy, ay my body for to kepe.

Valerian, while no Christian, apparently knew better than to challenge his wife's guardian angel. He therefore replied that if she would demonstrate to him that the angel was of God, he would respect her vow.

Cecilia sent him to see Bishop Urban, who was working among the Christians in the catacombs. Urban found Valerian to be a ready convert. The young man made a vow of chastity, was baptized, and returned to his pious wife. On his return, Valerian, along with his brother Tiburtius, beheld the angel who hovered over Cecilia. Their conversion was now complete.

The three young people dedicated themselves to good works—helping the persecuted and burying the martyrs. It was not long before Valerian and Tiburtius were arrested and brought to trial for their activities. A Roman prefect condemned them to be burned to death.

Cecilia, undaunted, continued her works of charity and was herself called before the prefect and warned to desist and to repudiate her beliefs. Rather than be more discreet, she sought to convert all who visited her. She opened her house to Bishop Urban, who baptized over four hundred people there.

Like her husband and brother-in-law, Cecilia was condemned to die. Her judge, Almachius, was reportedly angered that he could not seize her property since she had given it all to the poor. The means of execution was to be death by suffocation in her bathroom. Roman soldiers heated the furnace many times hotter than usual, but without causing Cecilia any harm. Finally, a soldier was dispatched to behead her. Even this attempt was not immediately successful. He struck her three blows to the neck without killing her, and since the law forbade more than three attempts, she was left to die slowly. She lingered for three days (during which time she had occasion to testify to concerned friends and neighbors) and finally died and was buried in the catacombs of St. Callistus.

The legend of Cecilia makes lively reading, but unfortunately it has no basis in fact. Nonetheless, to Roman Catholics she remains one of the most celebrated virgin martyrs and is the patron saint of music. In fact, although scholars strongly doubt her story, when the Roman Catholic liturgical year and calendar were revised in 1969, Cecilia's feast remained because of her popularity.

Cecilia's one claim to authenticity is a church in Trastevere, Rome, founded by a Roman matron named Cecilia. Other than that, our information consists entirely of fifth-century legend. Interestingly, there is no mention of Cecilia in the fourth-century *Depositio Martyrum*, nor does she appear in the writings of Ambrose, Jerome, or other near-contemporaries, all of whom had a particular interest in early Christian martyrs.

As with most Roman Catholic "saints," Cecilia has not been allowed any dignity in the grave. Her supposed remains have been dug up, examined, and venerated. In the ninth century, Pope Paschal moved her relics from the catacombs to a church in Rome. When the church was rebuilt in 1599, her tomb was reopened. According to one incredible story, the body was found to be intact, although it disintegrated on contact with the air. A sculptor, Maderno, was present and professed to have seen the body before it disintegrated. According to him, Cecilia was "not lying upon her back like a body in a tomb, but upon the right side, as a maiden in her bed, her knees drawn together, and seeming to be asleep."

Maderno immediately started working on a life-size sculpture of the saint, which can be seen today in the Church of St. Cecilia in Rome. A replica was made to fill the space that was originally her gravesite in the catacombs.

Cecilia has been known as the patroness of music since the sixteenth century. The association of Cecilia with music was made undoubtedly because "she sang in her heart to the Lord" during her wedding. In art she is usually depicted with an organ or a lute. Although her legend credits her with introducing the organ, the first evidence of an organ in Western Europe is from the eighth century. Nor has she been neglected by men of letters. John Dryden wrote a "Song for St. Cecilia's Day," and Alexander Pope wrote "Ode for Music on St. Cecilia's Day." The famous legend of Cecilia is reproduced in the lines of "The Second Nonnes Tale" from the *Canterbury Tales* by Chaucer.

Christopher

Nearly everyone can recall having seen the small images of St. Christopher that dangle from the rear-view mirrors of many automobiles. This favorite saint is supposed to protect travelers, although it is doubtful whether Roman Catholic drivers have a better accident record than do their Protestant counterparts. At any rate, Christopher has been entrusted with this responsibility since the Middle Ages when the stories about him were compiled in *The Golden Legend*, a book by Genoese archbishop Jacob of Voragine. The book had wide appeal because of its amazing stories of the saints and explanations of religious festivals. So popular has Christopher been, that when the Catholic hierarchy decided in 1969 that there is no adequate proof that he ever existed and accordingly removed him from the church calendar, there was vigorous protest from various European countries, led, oddly, by film stars in Italy.

Be that as it may, the story is still engaging. A man named Christopher lived some time in the third century. According to Roman martyrology, he was a victim of persecution under Decius, who commanded that Christopher be first tortured by fire, then shot with arrows, and finally beheaded.

Certainly, a more complete account of Christopher's life and death would be interesting and probably edifying as well, but in lieu of any other facts, a medieval writer presented a fascinating fiction that has survived as the legend of St. Christopher. This legend has as its basis the name *Christopher*, which means *Christ-bearer*. Because Christopher bore the testimony of Christ, the legendary account makes him the bearer of Christ's physical body as well.

According to *The Golden Legend,* Christopher was a Canaanite of enormous stature (eighteen feet) and intimidating appearance. After serving the king of Canaan for a time, it occurred to Christopher that he would like instead to serve "the greatest prince that was in the world." He left Canaan and eventually was employed in the court of a king who was generally considered to be the world's greatest ruler. One day while he was with the king, a minstrel entertained them with a song in which he often referred to the devil. The king made the sign of a cross on his face at each reference to Satan. Puzzled, Christopher requested of the king the significance of his sign of the cross. The king replied, "Always when I hear the Devil named I fear that he should have power over me, and I garnish me with the sign that he grieve me not nor annoy me." Christopher was dismayed by the answer because he realized that there was someone greater than his master. He determined to leave the king and seek the devil.

He found the devil in a desert amidst a company of fierce knights. Christopher immediately pledged to serve him. Once, as he traveled a highway with the devil, they chanced to see "a cross erect and standing." When the devil saw the cross, he fled, making a detour into the desert. Once again Christopher was amazed at the effect of the cross on his master's behavior. He demanded the reason for the devil's fear. "Wherefore the Devil was constrained to tell him . . . 'there was a man called Christ which was hanged on the cross, and when I see His sign I am sore afraid and flee from it wheresoever I see it.' " Christopher replied that it was clear he had not yet found the greatest master. He purposed therefore to seek Christ.

In his quest he met a hermit in the desert who told him of Jesus Christ and instructed him to fast and pray. Christopher balked at fasting, for one his size needed a great deal of nourishment, and insisted he knew nothing of prayer. The hermit then suggested an alternative service: "Knowest thou such-and-such a river, where many be perished and lost? . . . Thou shalt be resident by that river, and thou shalt bear over all them that shall pass there, which shall be a thing right pleasing to our Lord Jesus Christ whom thou desirest to serve."

Christopher made his home near the river and spent his time assisting travelers across the water. On one occasion as he slept, he heard a child's voice saying, "Christopher, come out and bear me over." When Christopher lifted the child, he found him to be "heavy as lead," and he nearly drowned in the attempt to cross the river. On the other side, he addressed his passenger, "Child, thou hast put me in great peril; thou weighest almost as I had all the world upon me." The child then revealed himself to be Christ, who "created and made all the world" and, in fact, bore the world on his shoulders. As proof of the validity of his claim, the child told Christopher that his staff would bear flowers and fruit the next morning.

The sign was fulfilled, and Christopher journeyed to the city of Lycia, intending to testify of Christ there. Unable to understand the local language, he prayed for illumination. When he was able to communicate, he "went to the place where they martyred Christian men, and comforted them in our Lord."

Christopher prayed that his rod would bear flowers and fruit again as a sign to the unconverted people of the area. As a result of this miracle, eight thousand men believed.

The king sent knights to deliver Christopher to him. Christopher converted the knights as they carried out their errand. He then testified boldly before the king and refused to obey the king's command that he sacrifice to Lycia's pagan gods. For this he was committed to prison, and the knights whom he had converted were beheaded.

While in prison, Christopher was visited by two beautiful women, Nicaea and Aulina, who were sent to seduce him. Christopher went to prayer and not only succeeded in withstanding the temptation, but also converted the women.

When the king heard the report, he sentenced the two women and Christopher to death. Christopher was first beaten with iron rods, then tortured with a burning, red-hot iron. Then, because he escaped the tortures miraculously unscathed, he was tied to a stake and shot at by archers. To everyone's surprise, the arrows "hung in the air about, nigh him, without touching." The king, however, was struck in the eye and blinded. "To whom Christophers said, 'Tyrant, I shall die to-morrow. Make a little clay, mixed with my blood, and anoint therewith thine eye, and thou shalt receive health.' "

Christopher was beheaded, and "the king then took a little of his blood and laid it on his eye, and said, 'In the name of God and St. Christopher!' and was anon healed." After his sight was restored, the king "believed on God and gave commandment that if any person blamed God or St. Christopher, he should anon be slain with the sword."

From that story arose the notion that anyone looking at an image of Christopher would not suffer harm that day. Artists therefore created large statues or painting to be displayed near the doors of churches in order that the members of the congregation might see them and be protected. Among artists' favorite scenes are Christopher's conversing with the hermit and carrying Jesus on his back. He is also depicted with his flowering staff, or during his temptation by the two women and subsequent torture and death. Sometimes he is even shown with a mermaid, presumably because of his service to travelers across the river.

During the Middle Ages Christopher became the patron of travelers and was also invoked for safety from storms, plagues, and sudden death. During the Reformation and Counter Reformation, the cult of Christopher suffered from vigorous criticism. However, the appeal of the legend is so strong that interest in Christopher revived, especially recently for his role in the protection of motorists.

Interestingly, in an area of Paris, France, where Citroen cars are manufactured, there is a church dedicated to Christopher. Some motorists display plaques with the time-worn adage: "Behold St. Christopher and go thy way in safety."

Valentine

Perhaps the best-known name among all of the patron saints is Valentine. Alban Butler, whose oft-cited *Lives of the Saints* (1756-1759) is a monumental but uncritical compilation of history and legend, summarizes the traditional story of Valentine:

> Valentine was a holy priest in Rome, who, with St. Marius and his family, assisted the martyrs in the persecution under Claudius II. He was apprehended, and sent by the emperor to the prefect in Rome, who, on finding all his promises to make him renounce his faith ineffectual, commanded him to be beaten with clubs, and afterwards to be beheaded, which was executed on February 14, about the year 270.

This brief account sounds trustworthy enough, were it not for the fact that Roman martyrology mentions two Valentines, both of whom were supposed to have been decapitated on the same day. The one was a priest in Rome, the other a bishop of Terni, about sixty miles away. Since the stories of the two martyrs contain such striking similarities, it would seem only natural, and historically convenient, to assume that the bishop and the priest were the same person.

Valentine's connection with lovers and our contemporary practice of exchanging greeting stems from an old legend, which is delightfully romantic and illustrates too well how readily fiction may be substituted for reality, especially when the fiction is so much more interesting.

According to the legend, when the Roman emperor Claudius II (268-270) outlawed Christianity, Valentine was among those who aided persecuted Christians. Claudius also issued a decree forbidding Romans to marry, intending by his decree to eliminate strong family ties that would make Roman men unwilling soldiers. Valentine ignored the decree, encouraging young couples in the underground church to be wed secretly with his blessing. When Valentine's activity was discovered, the emperor had him imprisoned to await execution.

While in prison, Valentine made friends with his jailer's blind daughter, whose sight he miraculously restored. According to *Kemmish's Annual for 1797*, "From that time the Girl became enamoured of him, nor did he treat her affection with Contempt. . . . While in Prison being deprived of Books, he used to amuse himself with cutting curious Devices in Paper, on one of which he wrote some pious Exhortations and Assurances of love." He sent one of these to his keeper's daughter the morning of his execution and concluded the message with the words, "Your Valentine."

Other folklore surrounding Valentine associates him with epileptic sufferers. Frank Staff, in his book, *The Valentine and Its Origins*, says that "in some parts of Germany epilepsy used to be known as Valentine's sickness." However, Valentine's name continued to be associated, not with the "falling sickness" (epilepsy), but with falling in love and lovers.

Besides the fanciful Valentine legend, there are two other possible reasons for the association. In A.D. 496, 183 years after Christianity was made legal by Rome, Valentine's feast day was set on February 14. On February 15, Romans had traditionally celebrated Lupercalia, a pagan festival of love and fertility. As one of the rites of the festival, young Roman men put the names of girls in a box and drew partners to the festivities.

Thus, it is likely that when the feast of St. Valentine began to be observed instead of the pagan Lupercalia, some of the latter's more innocent customs, such as the drawing of names, were incorporated. Again quoting Staff: "When the early Christian fathers were busy obliterating pagan superstitions and dates by substituting those of the Christian belief, names of many of the martyred Saints were used to replace the old festivals. In this way St. Valentine, having suffered on the eve of Lupercalia, the 14th of February, was now to perpetuate for ever the memory of this festival of the return of Spring."

Farfetched as it may seem, there was also a connection between Valentine's Day and the popular medieval belief that birds selected mates in the middle of February. The earliest known reference to Valentine and the mating of birds is Geoffrey Chaucer's *Parlement of Byrddes*, which was probably written between 1370 and 1380. The forty-fifth stanza contains these lines:

For this was on Saint Valentine's Day
When every fowl cometh to choose his [mate],
Of every kind that men think may;
And that so huge a noise gan they make,
That earth and air and tree and every lake
So full was, that underneath was there space
For me to stand, so full was all the place.

By the sixteenth century, so many poets and bards had used the association of Valentine with lovers, be they bird or human, that we can assume the custom of choosing a valentine was already well established. The Paston Letters, an English family's correspondence that dates to the 1470s, refer to the practice. One of the letters is from the mother of a marriageable daughter to a Paston cousin inviting him to visit on Valentine's Day and make his proposal. The girl later addresses her newly betrothed suitor as her "right well-beloved Valentine."

In 1969 the Roman Catholic Church removed Valentine's name from its list of saints, saying that he may never even have existed. For someone who might not have existed, Valentine has certainly inspired his share of literature and customs. *The Oxford Dictionary of Saints* makes this comment: "Whatever the reason, the connection of lovers with St. Valentine, with all its consequences for the printing and retailing industries, is one of the less likely results of the cult of the Roman martyrs."

Lucy

"The glorious virgin and martyr St. Lucy" is described by Alban
Butler as "one of the brightest ornaments of the church of Sicily."
This paragon of virtue, whom we shall call a legend because of the
absence of any convincing factual information about her life, was
born near the end of the third century in the town of Syracuse in Sicily. Her parents were wealthy members of the Sicilian nobility. Lucy's
father died while she was an infant, and she was reared as a Christian
by her mother, Eutychia. That much information about Lucy seems
to be dependable history, at least.

Butler tells us that "by the early dispositions which Lucy received,
and the strong influence of divine grace, Lucy discovered no disposition but toward virtue, and she was yet very young when she offered
to God the flower of her virginity." However, she kept her childhood
vow of chastity a secret. When Lucy came of age, her mother, being ignorant of her vow, arranged a marriage for her with a young
pagan. Lucy, instead of arguing, devised a plan to avoid the union.
She persuaded her mother to accompany her on a trip to Catania,
where the mother and daughter joined in prayer at the tomb of St.
Agatha to ask particularly that Eutychia might receive healing from
a hemorrhage from which she had suffered for a long time. Eutychia
was restored to health at the tomb. Lucy took advantage of that moment to disclose to her mother her intention to remain a virgin and
distribute her goods to the poor. Eutychia, being in a receptive frame
of mind, was happy to accord her daughter permission to carry out
"her pious inclinations."

The young pagan to whom Lucy was to be married, on the other
hand, was not in a receptive frame of mind and took the matter of the

broken engagement to court. He was no doubt at least as concerned
with the loss of his future bride's property as he was with the forfeiture
of the bride herself. In a rage, he accused Lucy before the governor
of being a Christian. The persecution under Diocletian then being in
progress, the judge condemned Lucy to a fate worse than death—ex-
posure to the life of a brothel.

Lucy, however, when sentenced, could not be subjected to her punishment because "God rendered her immovable." The guards were
unable to carry her to the house of ill-repute. Nor were they able to
punish her by fire since God repeated the miracle of the three Hebrew children in her behalf. However, she did finally succumb to the
effects of a sword-thrust to her throat. She died in 304.

Her "Acts" are preserved in both Latin and Greek but are not historically sound. An English bishop, Aldhelm of Sherborne, who lived
at the end of the seventh century, lauded her in prose and poetry, but
those effusions are based on the unreliable "Acts."

Lucy's cult was widespread in Syracuse and elsewhere. During the
sixth century, she was honored at Rome among the illustrious virgin
martyrs, and her name was inserted into the canon of the Mass at
both Rome and Milan. Churches dedicated to her are still standing
in Rome, Naples, Venice, and England, and her feast appears on the
Roman Catholic calendar on December 13. Butler tells us that until
"the change of religion" occurred in England, that country kept her
festival as "a holiday of second rank, in which no work but tillage or
the like was allowed."

Naturally, many churches clamored for her relics. These were moved
from Syracuse to another location in Italy, and from thence to Metz.
Some of the remains were also conveyed to Constantinople and from
there back to Venice, where they are highly valued.

Lucy's name suggests light or lucidity, and it is perhaps because of
these associations that Lucy has become the saint to whom those ex-
periencing eye trouble appeal for healing. During the Middle Ages,
she inspired two legends. In one, Lucy's eyes were put out by a tyrant.
In another, Lucy tore them out herself to present them to an unwel-
come suitor who had admired her beauty. In both legends, the ending
is a happy one: Lucy's eyes are miraculously restored.

Lucy figures prominently in the art of the Middle Ages. She is usually pictured holding her eyeballs on a dish or on a stem.

The whole unlikely story does little to promote the credibility of
sainthood in general. It is a shame that a person like Lucy, who may

well have been an honorable Christian who died for her faith, should be discredited by unwholesome veneration and ridiculous fiction until nothing factual remains of her history. A story such as Perpetua's, preserved in her own and a contemporary's words, is edifying, but a complete fabrication, such as Lucy's, can only entertain.

Butler's words at the close of the section about Lucy provide a clue to this obsession of the Roman church with "non-saints." He wrote that "it is a matter of the greatest consequence what ideas are stamped upon the ductile minds of children, what sentiments are impressed on their hearts, and to what habits they are first formed." He suggests that if given proper examples to emulate, children will develop upright character. It is unfortunate that Roman Catholics cannot rely upon genuine life stories to accomplish the noble goal of character building. Bible-believers should take note, too, of the great untapped resource they have in the biographies of notable Christians. Church history teems with noble followers of the Lamb in all walks of life—missionaries, preachers, statesmen, scholars, doctors, and businessmen, to name a few—whose life stories not only inspire but also teach us how to serve our Savior with greater faithfulness.

Nicholas of Myra

With the exception of the Virgin Mary, there is no saint of Roman Catholic tradition who has been depicted more often in works of art, and whose name has been affixed to more churches, than Nicholas of Myra.

This most popular saint has been venerated since the sixth century, if not before, for the wide variety of good deeds he is supposed to have done. Unlike many Roman Catholic saints, he is not immortalized for his glorious martyrdom. Rather, he is remarkable, from infancy to death (and even after) for his zeal, innate goodness of character, and numerous miracles in behalf of many classes of people. Like most other Roman saints, however, he is largely the product of imagination. The one fact about Nicholas that seems to be reliable, although it cannot be proven by any historical document, is that he lived in the fourth century and served as bishop of Myra, a city Paul had visited on his way to Rome (Acts 27:5). The first indisputable reference to him is the name of a church in Constantinople, built by the emperor Justinian in the sixth century.

Facts aside then, we turn to tradition and legend for the fascinating, if fictional, account of a much beloved saint, Nicholas.

He was born at Patara in Lycia (southwestern Turkey) to a young couple whose names were Epiphanes and Johane. Legend attests that "he was exceedingly well brought up by his parents and trod piously in their footsteps. The child, watched over by the Church . . . kept untarnished the innocence of his heart." As evidence of his piety, the absurd legend says he kept the church fasts as an infant, since he received his mother's milk only once on Wednesdays and Fridays, those feedings being in the evening, "according to the canons." At age five he is said to have shown great interest and progress in sacred learning.

At some point during Nicholas's boyhood, the episcopal seat at Myra, the capital city close to the coast, was left vacant at the death of its bishop. A group of bishops met to elect a replacement. One of them heard a voice in the night that instructed him to watch the door of the church that night and the first person to come to the door having the name of Nicholas should be made bishop. Accordingly, "at the hour of matins, like as he had been sent from God, Nicholas arose tofore [before] all others." The bishop announced the boy's new office on the spot and "brought him to the church, howbeit that he refused it strongly, yet they set him in the chair. And he followed, as he did tofore in all things, in humility and honesty of manners." About his deportment as bishop, the account continues: "He woke in prayer and made his body lean, he eschewed company of women, he was humble in receiving all things, profitable in speaking, joyous in admonishing, and cruel in correcting."

Some records assert that when Nicholas assumed the office of bishop at Myra, he endured persecution under the Emperor Diocletian. "As he was the chief priest of the Christians of this town and preached the truths of faith with a holy liberty, the divine Nicholas was seized by the magistrates, tortured, then chained and thrown into prison with many other Christians." However, when Constantine came to power, they were released, and Nicholas was at liberty to return to Myra.

Another historical event with which Nicholas is sometimes connected is the Council of Nicaea in 325. Nicholas was one of the 318 church fathers who met to condemn the Arian heresy. So zealous was Nicholas in rebutting the heretics that during a heated debate he struck an Arian bishop. (Some traditional accounts say it was Arius himself, although Arius was not a bishop and was not seated with the 318 leaders at Nicaea.) Nicholas was officially censured for his misconduct and was deprived of his office and put in prison. However, a miraculous intervention of the Lord and Mary secured his release and restored him to his position in Myra.

Nicholas was no less zealous against heresy at home. One historian, an eighth-century monk, Methodius, wrote, "Thanks to the teaching of St. Nicholas, the metropolis of Myra alone was untouched by the filth of the Arian heresy, which is firmly rejected as death-dealing poison."

Nicholas was also on the warpath against paganism. As part of his campaign he destroyed the temple of Artemis, the principal deity of his district. He also broke her images and converted the people from idolatry.

Nicholas's parents died when he was a young man, leaving him well-to-do. Rather than to enjoy his wealth, he devoted it to charitable causes. The first opportunity for distributing his riches arose when a neighbor, a nobleman who had become impoverished, despaired of finding husbands for his three unmarried, dowerless daughters. The poor father had arrived at the conclusion that he would have to abandon them to prostitution in order to provide for them. "And when the holy man Nicholas knew hereof he had great horror of this villainy, and threw by night secretly into the house of the man a mass of gold wrapped in a cloth." When the man awoke and found the gold, he thanked God for the gift, "and therwith [sic] he married his oldest daughter."

Nicholas delivered similar parcels at intervals for the other two daughters, who in turn were married. The grateful father awoke during Nicholas's final visit and called to his benefactor: "Sir, flee not away so but that I may see and know thee." He ran after Nicholas and discovered his identity, but "the holy man . . . required him not to tell nor discover this thing as long as he lived." We must assume that the father did not follow Nicholas's directive to secrecy, for the legend of the dowerless maidens is perhaps the best known of all the Nicholas folklore.

The legends featuring Nicholas are replete with threes. In addition to the three dowerless sisters, there is also the tale of three schoolboys who, on their way home, stopped to lodge at an inn. During the night, the innkeeper murdered them and threw their bodies into the brine tubs used for pickling meat. In the morning, Nicholas arrived to rebuke the wicked innkeeper and to restore the three boys to life.

Another story of threes is the legend of the three prisoners. The governor, Eustathius, had been bribed to condemn to death three innocent men. At the time of the execution, Nicholas stayed the executioner's hand and rescued the prisoners. He remonstrated with the corrupt governor until he repented. On the occasion of his penance, there were three imperial officers present who were en route to Phrygia. Later, in Constantinople, the three officers were themselves imprisoned unjustly by the prefect Ablavius, who wasted no time obtaining a death warrant for them from Constantine.

The officers, who had been greatly impressed by the influence Nicholas had wielded over his governor in a similar circumstance, prayed to God that Nicholas might appeal to Constantine to save them. That night Nicholas appeared in dreams to both the prefect Ablavius and the emperor Constantine, threatening them and demanding the release of the three officers. In the morning the three men were called in for questioning and revealed that they had prayed for Nicholas's intervention. Constantine then set them at liberty and sent the men to Nicholas with a letter asking him to pray for the peace of the world.

Nicholas is often associated in legend with storm-tossed mariners, for he is supposed to have miraculously brought safely to port a ship on which he was traveling to Palestine. It was not uncommon in some parts of Europe in centuries past to refer to a "star of St. Nicholas," or for sailors to say to each other, "May St. Nicholas hold the tiller."

Tradition says that Nicholas died in "the year of our Lord three hundred and forty-three, with great melody sung of the celestial company." He was entombed in his cathedral in Myra until 1087, when his relics were taken by Italian merchants to Bari, in southeastern Italy.

His death did not mark the end of his career as a miracle worker. Legend assures us that pilgrims to his shrine found that his "venerable body . . . embalmed as it was in the good ointments of virtue, exuded a sweet-smelling 'myrrh,' which kept it from corruption and proved a health-giving remedy against sickness." The removal of his remains from Turkey to Italy apparently did not disturb their healing properties because pilgrims continued to attest to the benefits of beholding the "manna of St. Nicholas."

By the sixth century there was already a large cult of St. Nicholas, and in the eleventh century, when his body was removed to Italy, his popularity spread even farther. Such was his renown that a Greek writer of the tenth century could say that "the West as well as the East acclaims and glorifies him. Wherever there are people . . . his name is revered and churches are built in his honor."

The various legends about Nicholas were favorite subjects for art by Europe's best masters. Because of the diversity of the stories about him and the types of people with whom he associated, he became the patron saint of children, sailors, maidens, merchants, pawnbrokers, apothecaries, perfumers, and others, including thieves! Nicholas's emblem in art is three gold balls (also the symbol for pawnbrokers—perhaps therein lies that unlikely association), which probably typify the three parcels of gold Nicholas delivered to the dowerless maidens. Nicholas is also the patron saint of many European cities and of the countries of Russia and Greece. In fact, two czars took his name, and ironically, Nikita Khrushchev's first name is a diminutive form of it.

Customs, based on legends about his life, abounded in the Middle Ages. One of these is the choosing of a Boy Bishop on Nicholas's traditional feast day, December 6. The boy, who was dressed regally and paraded through the streets, "reigned" until December 28. By the thirteenth century, December 6 was a gift-giving day.

The metamorphosis of Nicholas of Myra into Santa Claus of Christmas is a great transformation produced by many influences. The proximity of Nicholas's feast day to Christmas and the gift-giving traditions of both days made the association natural. In the European tradition, however, Nicholas was still represented as a solemn saint and bishop, lean rather than fat. The change occurred in America, specifically New York, in the early 1800s. The Dutch had transformed the name *Sinta Nikolaus* into *Sinterklaes*, hence Santa Claus, and they brought this with them when they settled New York in the 1600s. In 1809 Washington Irving wrote a good-natured satire on the Dutch in colonial New York, which he entitled *Diedrich Knickerbocker's History of New York*. The frequent reference he made to Nicholas and Santa Claus inspired two poems about him, "The Children's Friend" (1821) and "A Visit from St. Nicholas" (1822), later known as "The Night Before Christmas." The former introduced the sleigh drawn by a single reindeer, while the latter, written by an Episcopal clergyman named Clement C. Moore, multiplied the reindeer and likened Nicholas to the fat and jolly Dutchmen—with flowing white beard, red costume, and wide leather belt—that had filled Irving's book. Somehow Nicholas also became associated with the myth of Kriss Kringle, a Norwegian figure who gives gifts on Christmas Eve and whose name means "Christ-child." The American familiarity in a national sense with this new Santa Claus did not come until after 1863 when the magazine *Harper's Weekly* began including a picture of him each Christmas by the famous cartoonist Thomas Nast.

In 1969 the names of Nicholas and many other saints were removed from their traditional places on the Roman Catholic calendar and are now combined to be venerated on January 1.

Wenceslas

Good King Wenceslas looked out,
On the Feast of Stephen,
When the snow lay round about,
Deep, and crisp, and even:
Brightly shone the moon that night,
Though the frost was cruel,
When a poor man came in sight,
Gathering winter fuel.

"Hither, page, and stand by me,
If thou know'st it, telling,
Yonder peasant, who is he?
Where and what his dwelling?"
"Sire, he lives a good league hence,
Underneath the mountain:
Right against the forest fence,
By Saint Agnes' fountain."

"Bring me flesh, and bring me wine,
Bring me pine logs hither;
Thou and I will see him dine,
When we bring them thither."
Page and monarch forth they went,
Forth then went together;
Through the rude wind's wild lament,
And the bitter weather.

"Sire, the night is darker now,
And the wind blows stronger;
Fails my heart, I know not how,
I can go no longer."
"Mark my footsteps, good my page!
Tread thou in them boldly;
Thou shalt find the winter's rage
Freeze thy blood less coldly."

In his master's steps he trod,
Where the snow lay dinted;
Heat was in the very sod
Which the saint had printed.
Therefore, Christian men, be sure,
Wealth or rank possessing,
Ye who now will bless the poor,
Shall yourselves find blessing.
–John Mason Neale (1818-1866)

This song, "Good King Wenceslas," is often heard during the Christmas season, but few people know anything about the "good king" of whom they sing.

The song is based on one of the numerous legends surrounding Wenceslas, patron saint of Czechoslovakia (known since 1993 as Slovakia and the Czech Republic). Though his life is clouded by myths, as have been the lives of other historical figures canonized by the Roman Catholic Church, Wenceslas was nonetheless a very real person whose good deeds during his reign as prince of the Czechs earned him a "saint's" reputation. It is good deeds alone for which we salute him. There is no record of a conversion experience.

Wenceslas was born in 907 at Stochov, near Prague. His father, Ratislav, who ruled as duke from 915 until 920, hailed from a tribe already "Christianized." Wenceslas's mother, Drahomira, was the daughter of a prince of the heathen Lutices, a tribe in what is now eastern Germany. She became regent for Wenceslas, who was only thirteen when Ratislav died.

Young Wenceslas and a brother, Boleslav, were sent to the estate of their paternal grandmother, Ludmilla (also sainted by Rome), to be educated. Under her tutelage, Wenceslas became very devout, his piety becoming so well known that pagan nobles in the area feared that he would grow up to "become a monk rather than a ruler." In 921 Drahomira, who resented the influence Ludmilla exerted over Wenceslas, conspired with the nobles to have her murdered. Conflict between Christian and pagan factions did not end with the death of Ludmilla. Drahomira's ambition for power, court intrigues, and continuing political strife prompted Wenceslas to take over the reins of government that were rightfully his. He assumed leadership in 922.

Wenceslas's seven-year reign was notable for its policy of peaceable relations with bordering countries, although this policy was not enacted at the expense of strong defense. His newly organized army was not, however, ready to repulse an invasion by the German armies under Henry I, the Fowler, in 929. Rather than risk the inevitable devastation of his country by a clearly superior military power, Wenceslas agreed to pay yearly tribute to the German Empire.

Among his other political accomplishments was his reform of the judicial system, which before Wenceslas was "somewhat primitive," with the "judges apt to pass sentence arbitrarily." Wenceslas encouraged a reduction in the number of death sentences. A common symbol of this was a picture of the king cutting down the gibbets.

Legends also grew up about him because of his support of missionary effort during his reign, evidenced by the building of many stone churches. Tenth-century histories affirm that "priests came in great numbers from Bavaria and from Swabia with relics of the Saints and very numerous books. Wenceslas bestowed upon them gifts of gold and silver, beautiful ornaments, and even clothes and other such things as they had need of."

No aspect of his character has been more romanticized than his concern for the poor. Murals on Czech church doors depict Wenceslas helping women reap wheat in the fields. Legends relate that Wenceslas's habit was to cut wood or supply food secretly for widows and orphans, often carrying the provisions to them through the snow on cold nights.

His "saintly character" has also been heralded in legend:

> During Lent, and even in winter it was his custom to go barefoot over the steep and icy paths . . . to visit the churches of Christ, and people saw the blood-stained footprints that he left behind him. In order to preserve the chastity which he had vowed he wore a haircloth.

Beneath the magnificent robes of royalty he wore a wollen [sic] garment like a simple monk, thus shining equally before God and man. He took but little food, passed much of the night in vigils and continuously rendered thanks to God.

Wenceslas's influence apparently did not extend to his brother Boleslav and other nobles who remained pagan and rebellious under Christian rule. In September 929, Boleslav invited his ruler-brother to his residence for a banquet and then had Wenceslas murdered the next day, September 28, on his way to church.

Almost from the date of the murder, Wenceslas was hailed a martyr. September 28 is celebrated by Roman Catholic as his feast day, and the church, St. Vitus Cathedral in Prague, where his remains are interred, has been a famous pilgrimage site for Catholics through the centuries.

Selected Bibliography

Attwater, Donald. *A Dictionary of Saints.* Middlesex, England: Penguin Books, 1965.

Bainton, Roland Herbert. *Women of the Reformation.* Minneapolis: Augsburg Publishing House, 1977.

Bartlett, David W. *Joan of Arc.* Philadelphia: Henry T. Coates and Company, 1854.

Baur, Chrysostomus. *John Chrysostom and His Time.* London: Sands, 1959.

Bettenson, Henry, ed. *The Later Christian Fathers.* London: Oxford University Press, 1970.

Bishop, Morris. *Saint Francis of Assisi.* Boston: Little, Brown, and Co., 1974.

Boase, Thomas Sherrer Ross. *St. Francis of Assisi.* Bloomington: Indiana University Press, 1968.

Bonner, Gerald. *St. Augustine of Hippo.* Philadelphia: Westminster Press, 1963.

Brown, Peter Robert Lamont. *Augustine of Hippo.* Berkeley: University of California, 1967.

Bush, R. Wheler. *The Life and Times of Chrysostom.* London: Religious Tract Society, 1885.

Butler, Alban. *The Lives of the Fathers, Martyrs, and Other Principal Saints.* Dublin: R. Coyne, 1833.

Chabannes, Jacques. *St. Augustine.* Garden City, New York: Doubleday, 1962.

Cox, Raymond L. "Was St. Patrick a Protestant?" *Christian Life,* March 1969, pp. 24ff.

Cutts, Edward Lewes. *Saint Jerome.* London: Society for Promoting Christian Knowledge, 1897.

Davidson, John Norman. *Jerome: His Life, Writings, and Controversies.* New York: Harper and Row, 1975.

Deen, Edith. *Great Women of the Christian Faith.* New York: Harper and Brothers, 1959.

Delaney, John J., and Tobin, James Edward. *Dictionary of Catholic Biography.* Garden City, New York: Doubleday, 1961.

Dewar, Michael W. "Was St. Patrick a Protestant?" *Christianity Today,* March 4, 1957, pp. 3-4.

Dvornik, Francis. *The Life of Saint Wenceslaus,* Prague: State Printing Office, 1929.

Encyclopaedia Brittanica, 1981.

Encyclopedia Americana, 1979.

Encyclopedia International, 1978.

Englebert, Omer. *Saint Francis of Assisi.* New York: Longmans, Green, 1950.

Farmer, David Hugh. *The Oxford Dictionary of Saints.* Oxford: Clarendon Press, 1978.

Fines, John. *Who's Who in the Middle Ages.* New York: Stein and Day, 1970.

Fortini, Arnaldo. *Francis of Assisi.* New York: Crossroad, 1981.

Gilson, Etienne Henry. *The Mystical Theology of Saint Bernard.* New York: Sheed Ward, 1955.

Goudge, Elizabeth. *My God and My All.* New York: Coward-McCann, 1959.

Graham, Gabriela Cunningham. *Santa Teresa.* London: Eveleigh Nash, 1907.

Guardini, Romana. *The Conversion of Augustine.* Westminster, Maryland: Newman Press, 1960.

Guillemin, Henri. *Joan, Maid of Orleans.* New York: Saturday Review Press, 1973.

Hole, Christina. *Saints in Folklore.* New York: M. Barrows and Company, 1965.

Jackson, Samuel Macauley, ed. *The New Schaff-Herzog Encyclopedia of Religious Knowledge.* New York: Funk and Wagnalls Company, 1910.

James, Bruno S. *Saint Bernard of Clairvaux.* New York: Harper, 1957.

New Catholic Encyclopedia, 1967.

Sackville-West, Victoria Mary Nicolson. *Saint Joan of Arc.* New York: Literary Guild, 1936.

_____. *The Eagle and the Dove.* Garden City, New York: Doubleday, 1944.

Schaff, Philip. *History of the Christian Church.* 8 vols. New York: Scribner, 1893.

_____. *Saint Chrysostom and Saint Augustin.* London: James Nisbet, 1891.

Scherer, James Augustin Brown. *Four Princes.* Philadelphia: Lippincott, 1903.

Staff, Frank. *The Valentine and Its Origins.* New York: Praeger, 1969.

Stolpe, Sven. *The Maid of Orleans.* London: Burns and Oates, 1956.

Storrs, Richard Salter. *Bernard of Clairvaux.* New York: C. Scribner's Sons, 1892.

Teresa of Jesus. *The Life of St. Teresa of Jesus of the Order of Our Lady of Carmel, Written by Herself.* Trans. David Lewis, ed. Benedict Zimmerman. Westminster, Maryland: The Newman Book Shop, 1947.

Thurston, Herbert, and Attwater, Donald, eds. *Butler's Lives of The Saints.* New York: P. J. Kennedy and Sons, 1956.

Townsend, Reginald T. "On the Trail of Good King Wenceslas." *Country Life,* December 1929, pp. 73-74.

Willey, John Heston. *Chrysostom: The Orator.* New York: Eaton and Mains, 1906.

Wirt, Sherwood. "God's Darling." *Moody Monthly,* February 1977, p.56.

Index